MANAGING PEOPLE

by Gill Taylor & Christine Thornton

2003

06

04

5

A Directory of Social Change publication

D0599770

MANAGING PEOPLE

by Gill Taylor & Christine Thornton

Published by The Directory of Social Change
24 Stephenson Way, London NW1 2DP
Tel: 0171 209 5151, *Fax:* 0171 209 5049
e-mail: info@d-s-c.demon.co.uk
from whom further copies and a full publications list are available.

The Directory of Social Change is a Registered Charity no. 800517

First published 1995, reprinted 1997

ISBN 1 873860 47 1

British Library Cataloguing in Publication Data
A catalogue record for this book is available from the British Library

Cover design by Kate Bass
Designed and typeset by Paul Ticher
Printed and bound by Page Bros., Norwich

Other Directory of Social Change departments in London:
Courses and Conferences *tel:* 0171 209 4949
Charity/Charity Centre *tel:* 0171 209 1015
Research *tel:* 0171 209 4422
Finance and Administration *tel:* 0171 209 0902

Directory of Social Change Northern Office:
3rd Floor, Federation House, Hope Street, Liverpool L1 9BW
Courses and Conferences *tel:* 0151 708 0117
Research *tel:* 0151 708 0136

CONTENTS

Introduction

Section 1
Supervision

Section 2
Planning and team work

Section 3
Dealing with difficult situations

Section 4

Management Committee

Section 5

Letting staff go in difficult circumstances

ABOUT THE AUTHORS

Gill Taylor

is the senior management consultant of Connections Partnership, specialising in personnel and equality management. She has 12 years' experience of working in and consulting to the voluntary sector. Her particular interests are: working with directors and committees to design effective roles and jobs in organisations; working with teams on managing diversity and managing conflict. She has written several other books on personnel and equal opportunities.

Christine Thornton

works as a management development consultant with voluntary and arts organisations, to facilitate effective change and to develop managers. She has 15 years' voluntary sector experience including hands-on management and a management development role for a major network. Christine works from a dynamically-based understanding of individual, group and organisational life, and balancing the needs of all stakeholders. She has written several books including *Managing to Advise*.

INTRODUCTION

When you are new to management, management skills can seem like a mysterious well of insider knowledge. We all have our ideas of good and bad managers — but how well am *I* doing? What is a management style? and what is mine? Should I be more authoritative or less?

WHY THIS BOOK?

This book is aimed at those new to management and those working in small organisations or unsupported management positions.

It aims to demystify the skills involved in managing people, by looking at some fairly typical difficulties that face managers from time to time. You would be pretty unlucky to come across all of them! The approach is designed to help you improve your skills as you dip into it and lead to better management practice.

We intend it to be a source of good practice: you can pick it up when you face a difficulty and see how another manager coped with a similar problem.

The book is divided into five main sections: supervision, planning and teamwork, dealing with difficult situations, the management committee, and staff leaving in difficult circumstances.

STRUCTURE OF THE BOOK

In total there are 30 scenarios of different management problems that are regularly faced by managers. At the end of each main section is a resource and information page with references mainly applicable to that section. We chose to write in scenarios, attempting to replicate real life situations that managers face, for three main reasons:

- It makes the subject interesting and lively.
- It may strike a direct chord from your own experience.
- The dilemmas are 'real' rather than academic.

BACKGROUND TO THE SCENARIOS Each scenario follows the managers through the actions they take to deal with the issue and shows what options they might have had and the consequences of the actions they took.

There are three managers of different organisations and their teams featured in the book. While each scenario is self-contained, some of the scenarios follow on from each other taking the same characters working through a problem or issue over time.

CARLA

is the head of *HEALTH YOUTH ACTION*: an ex-midwife now running a small health promotion unit for young people based in a portacabin in the grounds of the Royal Infirmary. HYA is affiliated to the national *Organisation of Health Promotion,* but Carla is not directly managed by them. She reports to a local Management Committee. She manages three staff:

- 1 part-time secretary and admin worker: Alexis
- 2 health promotion workers: David and Kwame

SIMON

is the manager at *HOME ENERGY*: an advice centre on saving heat and energy in the home. They have a small shop front office in the centre of the town. He manages six staff:

- 3 energy advisers: Robina, Carlos, Marcia
- 1 secretary/administrator: Rose
- 1 publicity/promotions/information person: Leah
- 1 part-time finance worker 16 hrs per week: Jasvinder

MAGHIRA

manages a small Asian *FAMILY SUPPORT CENTRE.* She has a lot of pressure on her from funders and the community to deliver a wide range of services. Harbinder is chair of the Management Committee. The Centre has only four staff:

- 2 outreach workers: Pratibha, Shakti
- 1 children's support worker: Surinder
- 1 administration/finance worker: Kamlesh

In today's increasingly complex world, it is important that your organisation is able to change and adapt: for example, to new funding arrangements, to new requirements of the client or user or to new technology.

ORGANIS-ATIONS THAT CAN ADAPT AND CHANGE

Managing in a changing environment requires skills that are bound up with good personnel management. In a small voluntary organisation people are almost always your most important resource, so using them well is a key issue. And if our work is intended to improve the quality of life for users, how can we do this if we don't treat our staff well?

THE HIGH-PERFORMING ORGANISATION

A high-performance culture is the kind of culture that managers need to work towards to make their organisation most effective. Individual needs are important when you are working to achieve *quality* in your service. Organisations whose organisational climate achieves this balance of internal and external factors, are likely to be the most effective.

Characteristics of high-performing organisations:

- Concern for the future
- Concern to develop people in the organisation
- A focus on the service being provided
- An orientation to the technologies in use
- A concern for quality, excellence, service and competence
- An orientation to 'outsiders': users, clients, customers, the community
- Constant adaptation of reward systems and values
- Openness to new ideas

The corollary of these factors for the organisation:

- Lack of status differentials
- Innovation
- Sharing of responsibility
- Expression of feelings and needs
- Collaboration
- Open, constructive conflict
- Feedback
- Flexible leadership
- Involvement
- Trust

MANAGING PEOPLE EFFECTIVELY Effective people management has been defined as:

> 'a series of actions which enable working people and their employers to agree about the objectives and nature of their working relationship and to ensure that the agreement is fulfilled.'

It is about making sure that the work in the organisation is divided up in the most productive way, carried out to meet quality targets and that any difficulties in carrying out the task are resolved as quickly and fairly as possible. It is also about ensuring the team works well together, that all member's roles are valued and styles of working supported (provided they get the job done).

The main management skills:
- Defining jobs and roles
- Making sure the job gets done as well as possible
- Supporting problem solving and dialogue
- Team leadership
- Dealing with difficulties
- Listening and feedback skills
- Patience

Defining jobs and roles

An organisation has to divide up the tasks into sensible packages to get the work done by people who have the skills needed to do it. In small organisations this may be problematic as there are so few employees; everyone has to be something of a generalist. However there are definitely some combinations that are unlikely to go well together as the skills needed are radically different. Although many organisations put these roles together, experience shows that it is usually a mistake to combine:

- Fundraising with Finance
- Computer Manager with Personnel Manager
- Research with PR

Once job descriptions and person specifications have been written, then the manager has to recruit and select for the post in a fair manner following equal opportunities principles.

Making sure the job gets done as well as possible

When workers are in post they need support, supervision, training, development and appraisal, which also help the manager ensure that workers know what they must do and the standards that are expected of them in carrying out the tasks. If work and standards are not defined closely enough, then workers can become either demotivated or overburdened. It is important to do this work to get the best out of your team.

Supporting problem solving and dialogue

Within the team it is up to you to support people's ability to make decisions, and to set priorities and strategies for action. If team members are not able to get on, or if they do not have the skills to negotiate assertively, then you need to encourage them by example and perhaps by sending them on training courses. Good managers help their teams to get to know each other and to learn to trust, respect and appreciate individual talent and ability.

Conflict within the group is normal and inevitable. It is good practice to listen to all sides of the debate and then work to resolve it fairly and quickly before it can become destructive.

Team leadership

As the leader of the team, you must ensure that the activities it pursues are productive and the morale is positive. Seven ways in which you can do this are:

- Expect that all employees will meet their quality standards for their work, but give the personal attention needed to help with any shortfalls.
- Keep promises made to any team members.
- Be consistent and act positive even if you feel negative.
- Set a good example and support organisational policies and procedures.
- Stay calm under pressure — never swear at people!
- Provide opportunities to meet and share ideas.
- Make sure all goals are clearly communicated and understood.

Dealing with difficulties

When difficulties between people arise you need to sort them out — fast, either by working on the disputes between individuals or by using the disciplinary and grievance procedures if necessary. The longer you leave poor performance or incapacity, the more difficult the repercussions will be, for the individual, the team and the organisation.

Listening and feedback skills

Good managers are good at feedback, they know that the best feedback is specific and couched in a way that the recipient can hear it. When delivering critical messages it is especially important to let the person know how you feel about them. This helps honesty — and effective communication is always honest.

Patience

Finally — there will be times when you really want to blow your top, but good managers don't do it in front of the whole team. You explain how you are feeling and go off quietly somewhere to kick the refrigerator or something. Patience is definitely required in small voluntary sector teams.

Outbursts should be few and far between or people will classify you as a difficult person. If you do lose control then always apologise — not for feeling angry , but for your outburst.

Effective leadership

Generally an effective leadership style allows you to:

- Identify and target realistic and relevant goals
- Produce realistic and relevant results
- Align your goals to stated organisational goals
- Set performance requirements that are based on measurable items such as quality, cost, timeliness
- Revise plans as necessary
- Keep lines of communication open

*'Anyone can become angry — that is easy. But to be angry with
the right person, to the right degree, at the right time, for the right
reason and in the right way — that is not easy.'*   Aristotle.

There has been a lot written about management styles. The better **MANAGEMENT**
styles encourage people to participate in management action, **STYLES**
without being afraid to take a decision if there is no consensus.

The buck *does* stop with you (or you and the Management
Committee) — so you have to take the responsibility to act.

Styles which lead to poor decision making and increased stress on
the organisation include:

- **Authoritarian** — where the manager takes the decisions or tries
  to impose them without involving others.
- **Laissez Faire** — where the manager lets action take place in an
  undirected fashion reacting to crises as they occur.

You need to develop a style you feel comfortable with. A key
lesson is that some staff will push your boundaries *wherever* you
set them. Some people will do this for the hell of it, some simply
to clarify where the boundaries really lie. Your job is to hold the
boundaries where you have decided to set them.

Feeling confident

If you are feeling unconfident, here are some suggestions for
improving your confidence as a manager:

- Think before you speak and act.
- Get some training.
- Practise being authoritative even if you don't feel confident
  — it will come with practice.
- Encourage participative management, and practise
  delegating work effectively (but be clear which decisions
  stay yours).
- Discuss your management hassles and experiences with an
  outside supporter.
- Be there for your staff and they will reward you with good
  work.

If you are a manager who is black, a woman, or from a traditionally disadvantaged group you may find that some people (who feel threatened by you being in a position of power) will push you to see how far you can be pushed into a corner before you bite back. If you are in this position, is not your *fault*, but it is your problem to deal with it, not to let it slip.

THE MANAGER'S BALANCING ACT

Managers are always balancing something and under pressure to stretch scarce resources. Two difficult balancing acts which are common, especially in small organisations, are described below.

Stress — What to do if you feel out of control

Stress is covered in the scenarios, but we can't emphasise enough that it is imperative to deal with it before it gets out of hand. Managers in small voluntary sector projects are torn in all directions, routinely facing high stress. You often have to work very hard for little reward and with little access to support.

Please take the action we suggest when you hit your stress button — before it hits you with burn-out. Learn how to plan to offset high stress times, like funding applications and end of year returns. Take it seriously. You are not being a wimp in safeguarding yourself and your health.

Working with the Management Committee

This can often seem like the most difficult balancing act of all! The Management Committee may have knowledge and experience about the issues or concerns of the project, but they do not often have a lot of people with management experience. You may feel caught in the middle between the demands of staff, funders, committee and the work.

Try to find someone to support you, and do not expect huge amounts of support from the committee — they employed you to take work off their shoulders! The most practical option may be find informal support from other managers in a similar position to yourself, or to persuade the Management Committee to set up a formal arrangement for non-managerial supervision

Section 1
SUPERVISION

Scenarios

1 SETTING STANDARDS FOR PERFORMANCE

How to get good work from new staff — from the start

Alexis has been in post at *Health Youth Action* for two months as part-time secretary and administrator. She has had no formal training in secretarial or administrative skills. She was selected as being the best of the candidates on all round performance and good communication skills.

Carla, her director, recognised that she was rather weak on the secretarial side but she 'came over well' and seemed as if she would have a good manner on the telephone. Carla meant to organise proper training and induction, but has been landed with a large funding application *and* the end of the financial year *and* the Annual report all at the same time — so she has let it slip.

One of the other workers, Kwame has complained to Carla that he thinks Alexis is not producing letters to a 'professional standard'. He has complained more than once to Alexis and she has responded crossly with him. The standard of work has not improved. They both go to Carla separately and complain about each other!

OPTIONS Should Carla:

- Tell Kwame off for interfering when he isn't Alexis' supervisor?
- Discuss with Kwame first what he finds 'unprofessional' and help him to set boundaries to his management relationship with Alexis?
- Discuss the issue with Alexis first and set some guidelines herself?

COMMENT *Good management of performance relies on some basic groundwork being done to prevent problems either developing in the first place or getting out of hand subsequently. This starts at the recruitment and selection stage, and then requires sorting out standards and appropriate training once the worker is in post.*

TIPS for setting performance standards

- Clear tasks set out in the Job Description.
- Clear person specification identifying the skills needed to do the job.
- Good recruitment procedures that select the most competent person.
- Planned induction programme to familiarise staff with the detailed requirements of the job.
- Standards and guidelines written down for performance where applicable.
- Regular supervision of staff.
- Training and support as required to improve performance.
- Performance appraisal systems that benefit both the member of staff and the quality of the work.

ACTION

Carla decides to talk to Kwame first about the issue of Alexis' performance and the way in which he handled the problem.

Carla feels that he should have come to her when the situation seemed not to be resolving itself quickly; he is not in any formal supervision relationship with Alexis and has upset her by becoming impatient and criticising her standard of work. Carla tells Kwame that she wants him to tell Alexis about her good work as well as any sub-standard work and to give her feedback in a way in which does not alienate her. They also discuss some guidelines for Alexis' layout of letters.

Carla then discusses the issue with Alexis. She says what she has told Kwame about giving feedback — which helps to clear the air and allows Alexis to listen more constructively to the rest of the discussion.

Carla apologises about not organising training or being clear about how she wanted the work done before now. She sets out some clear guidelines for the layout of letters and reports, and they agree how long it should reasonably take to get letters sent out and reports typed. They discuss and agree a training course for Alexis to go on.

They also set a review date for monitoring how she is keeping up to these targets and agree that all the other workers should keep a record of work that she does for them and how long it takes to complete.

Over the next two months Carla has regular weekly supervision sessions with Alexis, for ½–1 hour. Carla is pleased that she can use the results of the monitoring system to show Alexis her progress and to give her some good feedback about her improving performance.

COMMENT *Induction and supervision are very important in getting new workers off to a good start and making relationships with colleagues easier. Tension could have been avoided between Kwame and Alexis much earlier on if Alexis had been given some ground rules and training. Carla made some wrong assumptions about Alexis' abilities and then did not support Alexis in trying to set and reach the required standards of performance.*

GENERAL ACTION TIPS

- Make sure you set good person specification standards for skills needed to do the job you are recruiting for. Be specific, but do not set them too high.

- Stick to the person specification when you are recruiting — no matter what the temptation to take someone who 'fits in' but doesn't have the required skills. This will result in frustrations and difficulties all round. It is important to recruit a person who will work well as part of your team, but they must have the requisite skills as well. So try to define closely what you mean by 'fitting in' in terms of team work and communication skills.

- Always test the skills that you can test for: typing, telephone manner, reception skills etc. This helps avoid nasty surprises when staff are in post.

- The importance of good and regular supervision cannot be overestimated. It helps you to nip problems in the bud before they get out of hand; motivates staff; leads to improved performance; creates better team relations.

- Don't let induction slip because you are too busy — it pays dividends in the long run.

WHAT CARLA MIGHT DO NEXT   Acknowledge the importance of good induction and regular supervision. Read up about supervision and write out an induction plan for new workers. Revise the person specifications to be more specific about any typing and layout skills required.

2 GIVING FEEDBACK

How to improve performance without giving offence

Simon is concerned about Robina, one of the three energy advisers. One or two users have said things that indicate that they find her difficult to deal with, though no one has made any specific complaint. Robina's advice is usually technically excellent, so the difficulty seems to be about how she behaves with people. Robina's manner is brisk and sometimes Simon has found her aggressive. He feels he needs to tackle the issue, but is not sure what to say, or how.

Should Simon:

OPTIONS

- Wait for Robina to mention something?
- Mention casually in the kitchen that he has heard there is a problem with her advice work, and see what she says?
- Check out further what the problem is?
- Wait until next week's supervision session, and introduce the topic then?

TIPS for good quality feedback

- Effective feedback or criticism offers a suggestion for change in a way that the other person can hear and accept.
- Try to give at least as much praise as criticism.
- When offering feedback, focus on the person's *behaviour*, what they do and say. Be very specific.
- Offer the other person the opportunity to put their side.
- Don't attribute motives, intentions or personality characteristics.
- Be as specific as possible about what *behaviour* you want in future.

ACTION Simon decides that he needs to clarify the issue further before tackling Robina. So he decides to speak informally to two or three discreet long-term users with whom Robina has worked. He remembers from a supervision course that in giving critical feedback it is important to ensure privacy, so will use the supervision session, not casual opportunities. He also decides to look again at his notes from the course!

Simon finds that some users feel that Robina does not respect them. He has sometimes felt that when he offers Robina feedback, positive or negative, she disregards it. Simon feels nervous about saying this to Robina, and realises that he must plan especially carefully how to handle the session, to set a positive context for the discussion.

He decides to:

- Welcome Robina and put her at ease; restate the purpose of supervision sessions — to review and plan work performance.
- Say how pleased he is with the technical quality of her advice.
- Ask how she feels about her energy advice giving and ask if there are any areas where she could improve her performance.
- If what she says allows him an opening, use it. If not, introduce the topic by saying that one or two users have felt hurt by her, and follow up by stating the problem: her *behaviour* — a tendency to interrupt when she feels that what users are saying is not relevant, and not always listening to what they say.
- Pause to allow or invite Robina to respond.
- Remind her that users feeling they are well treated is as important a part of the service as accurate assessment and advice.
- Make it clear how he wishes Robina to change her behaviour.
- Discuss what support she might need, for instance training, joint interviewing.
- Set realistic deadlines together to review this part of her performance.

OUTCOME Simon followed his plan for Robina's supervison session. At first she angrily refuted what he was saying, but Simon stayed calm, made his point again and refused to be drawn into conflict. He pointed out that Robina wasn't listening properly to what he was saying either.

She confided that she felt more confident analysing the energy problems than 'selling' the solutions to users, particularly older people. In the end she agreed to do some joint interviewing with Simon, to attend a course on 'active listening', and to review her interactions with users after two and six months. As she left she thanked Simon for his patience in listening to her.

Simon displayed the value of listening in the way he dealt with   **COMMENT**
Robina, which helped her to value it in her work with users.

GENERAL ACTION TIPS

- Remember that as a manager, your feedback is vital to maintaining your team's motivation, even if it feels difficult to do.

- Keep the context positive. Celebrate strengths and clarify shared service values which support your case.

- Make sure that difficult feedback is not rushed. Maintain a pace that allows time for the staff member to absorb and deal with the message.

- Don't get heated. Stay concrete and specific about what you want to be changed.

- Have clear ideas about what you want, but not about the means of getting it — listen to what the staff member says about her/his needs.

He could review the supervision session, to consolidate his own learning   **WHAT SIMON**
about what was effective and what was less so.   **MIGHT DO**
NEXT

3 MOTIVATION

Encouraging staff to do a good job

Simon is concerned because his staff, who are all pretty good at their jobs, seem rather unenthusiastic. He is keen to develop the service, integrating the casework and education work more, and doing a take-up campaign on some local grants.

He has tried to share his enthusiasm at a staff meeting, but has been met with an apathetic response. It's not that the team won't do the work, but that they are not offering suggestions about how to do it. He feels frustrated, because he knows that his staff really do care about the work, but he can't seem to engage their interest.

OPTIONS Should Simon:

- Give his team a good talking to?
- Ignore the problem and press on with his plans, hoping the team get more involved later?
- Ask them what the problem is?

TIPS about motivation

- No one is responsible for the motivation of another person. We motivate ourselves.

- Motivation is a very complex business, and managers cannot *control* the motivation of their staff. They can only act in the ways most likely to influence staff motivation for the good — or otherwise.

- People need to feel involved, and are most committed to goals which they have set or have had a say in setting.

- Enthusiasm is infectious where there are no barriers between people; unresponsiveness may be an early sign that there are blocks in communication or team work.

16

Simon is perplexed.   He mentions the problem to the Chair of the **ACTION**
Management Committee, and she suggests that maybe staff are feeling
overburdened, or that they feel that they have no contribution to make.
Apparently one or two staff have mentioned to a management committee
member that they have some difficulty with Simon's management style;
the committee member approached suggested that they raise the issue
first with Simon himself.

The Chair affirms Simon's basic approach and the excellent job that she
and the Management Committee feel he is doing. Simon is taken aback
and rather hurt at the fact that staff have spoken to Management
Committee members first rather than him, and realises that a
communication problem is beginning to develop between him and his
staff.

Simon knows that people's feelings at work are important — his *and* his
team's. He decides to raise the issue at the next staff meeting. He feels
he can trust his staff to be civil as well as honest, and can trust himself to
prevent things getting out of hand. He lets people know in advance that
he wants to raise 'a communication problem'. He opens by setting some
groundrules — that people can say what they really think as long as they
do so in a courteous way, and that everyone including him listens
carefully to what is said. He briefly describes his feelings about what has
happened so far.

After a bit of rather cynical grouching, the discussion gets down to the
real issues. Leah says that she has so much to do now that she cannot
think about development. Marcia says that she feels that she has no real
say in what *Home Energy* does: Simon's development proposals are
always so well thought through that she feels she has nothing to add.
And why does he need to bring plans to the staff meeting — after all, he
is the manager and will make the ultimate decision.

Others agree, and Robina adds that she is feeling at a personal dead end
— she does a good job but it is well within her capabilities: where can she
go next? Jasvinder suggest that they need some time together to talk
through how to plan their work and work more effectively together. He
thinks it would be a good idea to engage a facilitator to help them with
the process.

After the discussion, everyone is feeling much better. Simon realises that **OUTCOME**
the problems are not as critical as he feared; he believes that he should
act quickly to consolidate the goodwill now being expressed, and so
decides to act on Jasvinder's suggestion.

He finds that the training budget is under-committed; he prepares a brief for a consultant to work with him and the team to review their work and plan the next year's, and to help them look together at how they work as a team. He realises that he must involve the team at a much earlier stage in thinking through new work development — he can put the polish on plans later. He also decides to look into the whole area of staff development, which he thinks may help with the feelings that some staff have that they are personally stuck.

COMMENT *Simon's willingness to take the risk of asking his staff about their view of the problem, to listen to their answers and to act on what they say, contributed to a potentially positive outcome to the problem while it was still relatively easy to tackle. He is also willing to devote resources to looking after himself and the team properly (having a facilitator to manage the further discussion).*

GENERAL ACTION TIPS

- There is not always one simple problem with motivation. Take steps to address *each* problem.

- Where the problem is with the group not with an individual, address it on that level. Get help with managing the process if that would be helpful. (Management Committee members or colleagues from other organisations, as long as they have good group skills, are an alternative to paid consultants.)

- Listen carefully to what people say about their own motivation, and act on it.

- Working towards a goal and achieving it makes us feel good, and we are then *more* likely to set more ambitious goals the next time. Failing to achieve goals makes us feel bad and de-motivated.

- Involve people in setting work objectives to help maintain motivation through the 'feelgood factor'.

WHAT SIMON MIGHT DO NEXT Keep up the good work! And let the Management Committee know, in general terms, what is going on.

4 STAFF DEVELOPMENT

How to keep staff enthusiasm and increase skills

Simon has decided to look into staff development as a way of encouraging his very capable and experienced team members to stay motivated. His staff are advisers with highly developed and specialised skills, very valuable to the organisation — but only in one area. Some of them are wondering what their next step can be. There is almost no prospect of internal promotion, or of similar jobs in the area.

Should Simon: OPTIONS

- Talk more about long-term development in supervision sessions?
- Draw up a staff development policy?
- Let them go on lots of courses?
- Look actively for options which help broaden his staff's skills?
- Try to link personal development with organisational development?

TIPS on staff development

A staff development policy in action can:

- Help retain highly skilled staff who still perceive themselves as gaining learning.
- Keep staff interested and motivated.
- Complement organisational development and change.
- Be linked to NVQs and SVQs.

Simon looks into things further and finds that a staff development **RESEARCH** approach looks at individual interests as well as organisational needs, and takes a long-term view. His reading is mostly geared to larger companies which have more money than him, but he finds some useful principles. He feels that valuing staff for more than their immediate usefulness to the project is in tune with the values of *Home Energy*.

ACTION He decides to act on most of his options. Nevertheless his budget is limited. He decides that in choosing training, priority must be given to courses which develop the staff's ability to do their present jobs; after that, some resources can be spent on courses which develop skills which might be used in other jobs, either in *Home Energy* or elsewhere. He decides to set aside some of the training budget for these options.

Simon decides to act too on those development activities which don't cost money, but may cost some time, such as offering team members shadowing, visits, and the opportunity to share more tasks so as to develop new skills. One obvious area is on the pro-active publicity and information side, where Leah is feeling overburdened — so *Home Energy* can benefit too. He could also delegate some of his own work. Simon also considers the teamwork training that is planned with a facilitator as something that will help staff develop.

He develops a policy, with objectives, a statement that the policy applies to all staff, a budget and a set of priorities for spending the budget. He decides that the policy means that each person should be able to pursue at least one development opportunity a year, with priority use of money given to women and black staff, in line with the centre's Equal Opportunities policy.

OUTCOME Most staff greet Simon's proposals with enthusiasm, only pointing out that if some development activities cost time, then the time had to be allowed for in work planning. Simon accepts that this is necessary, but clarifies that there will be a upper limit to the time cost that the organisation can bear.

COMMENT *Voluntary organisations cannot afford to take too narrow a view of staff's development needs; the sector is far more inter-related than other sectors, as most staff have to move organisation if they seek promotion or other development. 'Casting bread on the waters' in this way is a good long-term investment for the sector as a whole — and staff who are still learning are more likely to stay.*

It is essential to have some budget for staff training. But money is often very limited, so concentrate too on development activities which cost time, not money.

GENERAL ACTION TIPS

Additional options include:

- Broadening roles/joint work
- Shadowing
- Visits to other organisations
- External supervision
- Unpaid sabbatical leave/time off for long-servers to pursue personal goals
- Skill-swapping with other organisations — staff are seconded/act as consultants
- Mentoring by senior staff in same or other organisations
- Conferences, advisory groups and campaign groups
- Allowing administrative staff to take up a wider role
- Effective use of delegation
- Membership of relevant professional bodies
- Representing the organisation in public

Work through in detail with individuals what he is actually offering, and look at expanding the range by considering some of the other options in 'General Action Tips'.

WHAT SIMON MIGHT DO NEXT

5 STAFF TRAINING

Developing a policy and getting the resources to implement it.

Two workers separately approach Maghira about going on training courses. Kamlesh wants to do a 10-week book-keeping course that will bring him up to NVQ level 3 costing £90, and Surinder wants to go on a 1-day child abuse seminar at £100.

Maghira realises that she has no mechanisms for deciding the relative merits of these requests, nor does she have a specific training budget or a training policy.

OPTIONS Should Maghira:

- Agree to both suggestions and work on a training policy later?
- Suspend all training until a policy is worked out?
- Consult with the treasurer on how much she can spend on training?

TIPS for organising training

- Making specific provision in the budget for staff training is a good idea to show the funders and good for staff planning and development.

- A training policy is a useful part of the staff procedures because it sets out the parameters for training within the organisation and gives staff a clear idea of what they can ask for or expect to get or be offered.

- Do not put off requests for training if you can afford them and you feel they are legitimately in the interests of improving staff skills. This would be bad for motivation and staff morale.

Maghira checks with the treasurer about spending the money.

She agrees to the two courses.

She starts researching ideas for a training policy to present to the Management Committee.

Once Maghira starts to think about a training policy and gets a draft down on paper that the staff can see, she begins to realise that it is not as easy as she first thought. **ISSUES**

- Does it apply equally to all staff?
- How do you choose between conflicting priorities for training?
- Does the money get divided equally by person or by organisational or individual need?

She discusses the issue at a staff meeting and then prepares a paper to go to the Management Committee.

Maghira has a policy to go to Management Committee which covers the following issues: **POLICY OUTCOME**

How and how often training needs of staff are assessed

Each year the co-ordinator will discuss with the staff their training needs for the following year (as part of performance appraisal — see following scenario). The resource implications can then be incorporated into the following year's budget.

Under what circumstances training can be offered to staff

Induction: Each staff member will receive appropriate training as part of their induction period — a standard programme and additional modules depending on which job the worker is doing.

Initial training: All new staff must receive the training necessary to enable them to carry out their jobs. This will take place as part of the induction and probationary period.

The initial training programme should be linked to the needs of the job description, person specification, and the individual's needs assessed in the light of what skills they bring to the post.

All initial training will include commitment to the equal opportunities, service delivery and customer care policies.

Continuing training: There will always be some need for staff members to receive training as part of the job. This could include new knowledge, computer programmes, practice developments, skills, attitudes or refresher training to match the requirements of the job that may change.

Staff development: Staff development is recognised as important for developing the skills base of the project and staff morale.

Whose responsibility it is to decide on training

It is the responsibility of the co-ordinator to draw up the individualised induction programme elements for each new staff person and to identify and address the training needs of staff. This should be done as part of regular supervision sessions with an emphasis on an annual audit as mentioned above to fit in with the annual budget.

How the training needs will be met

Once a training need has been identified and prioritised within the organisation the manager and the staff person should discuss ways to meet it.

This could include:

- coaching
- external courses
- in-house training
- attending conferences and training seminars
- access to women-only or black-only training for career development

Priority areas

Priority areas for training in order are:

- induction
- initial training
- continuing training
- staff development.

How conflicting demands will be dealt with

In considering continuing training and staff development,   the organisation's needs may lead to specific training for a particular staff member being prioritised; after this, preference should be given to those who have received less training in the past.

Maghira now has a comprehensive policy which will hopefully provide her **COMMENT**
with good guidance on allocating resources for staff training. She will be able to build the necessary resources into the next year's budget.

GENERAL ACTION TIPS

- Listen to a worker's career development plans and offer support if possible too.
- Talk in advance to workers going on external training, to emphasise the importance of the training to their job.
- Make sure the worker's tasks are done by someone else when they are on training so they are not worrying about work all the time.
- Make sure workers have an action plan to help apply their training to their job.
- Ask each worker for an evaluation of the training course.
- Remember to compliment workers on their newly learned skills.
- A budget of about £600 per worker is realistic.

Apply for a Women in Management development course.

**WHAT
MAGHIRA
MIGHT DO
NEXT**

6 PERFORMANCE APPRAISAL

De-mystifying appraisal for staff and managers

Carla hears from Alexis in the ladies loo that Kwame is getting agitated about his performance appraisal meeting next month. Alexis overheard him talking to David about it — "what to expect and would it affect his cost of living award". He hasn't had one before in his other jobs and is worried that he might not be able to 'impress' her.

Carla was hoping that she would have some more time to design the appraisal forms to improve them this year. They are rather perfunctory and are not really tailored enough for the health promotion side of the job. She got them from Central office last year when they sent an instruction that all staff were to have performance appraisals — but she was given no detailed guidance about how to do it.

OPTIONS Should Carla:

- Ignore the gossip and press on with sending out the old appraisal forms and covering letters to the staff?
- Phone the personnel advisor at head office and see if there are any standard forms and guidance which other health promotion teams have developed?
- Bring forward discussing the general issues about performance appraisal and set a deadline of two weeks before the appraisal dates to have a new form of more use than the old one?

APPRAISAL FORMS You need three kinds of appraisal form:

1. A **pre-appraisal form for the worker** to fill in which enables them to prepare for the appraisal by reflecting on their job, themselves, how things have gone or changed in the last year and how they might develop in the future, and their training needs.

2. A **pre-appraisal form for the manager** which details the areas of work from the job description and the skills from the person specification and enables the manger to score the performance of the worker against them.

3. An **appraisal interview form** covering a range of general points arising from the content of the work, how it is done, future plans and training needs, with some comments from the manager first and then discussion noted from both parties.

> ## TIPS on appraisal
>
> Staff appraisals are different from supervision sessions. They are usually longer, held every six months to a year, are more formal, and give an opportunity to reflect as well as to look forward.
>
> Appraisal is often thought of in the context of being related to pay awards. This is not usually the case in the voluntary sector. An appraisal system should enable each worker to:
>
> - Be clear about expectations of their performance.
> - Receive feedback from their manager on their performance.
> - Understand how their work ties up with and affects the work of others.
> - Identify development needs and career aspirations.
> - Inform the manager about changes to job description they feel are necessary.
> - Have the opportunity to exchange views and progress working relationships.

Carla phones head office, and they can send her forms that another **ACTION** Centre has developed, and on disc too. She is profoundly grateful.

She amends them slightly to include more relevant questions and comment for her workers.

She explains the forms in the next supervision session with each staff person.

She takes the time to go through the performance appraisal interview process in advance and thinks through her strategy with each employee.

OUTCOME   The appraisal interviews went well. They certainly benefited from the planning work that Carla put into designing the new forms to make them more relevant for her staff. She now has a blueprint for action over the next year and a training priorities schedule. Her staff are now much more relaxed and motivated, and perhaps won't be too difficult to manage for a while.

GENERAL ACTION TIPS

If you lack confidence go for appraisal interview training.

From the appraisal interview the manager should:

- Gain a clearer idea of the job being done, areas of competence, skill and achievements.
- Discuss work difficulties or potential difficulties.
- Set objectives and targets for the worker to achieve.
- Think further about their role in relation to the worker.
- Plan future training.

From the appraisal interview the worker should gain:

- A clearer understanding of the work performance, areas of competence, skill and achievements.
- A better idea of their role and how this fits into the whole organisation.
- A clear awareness of how their performance is assessed and therefore a better understanding of how to monitor their own performance in the future.
- The opportunity to raise questions and criticism in a constructive context.
- More understanding about future training and future development opportunities.

Managers themselves are often neglected in the appraisal process as the Management Committee may lack the skills or knowledge on personnel issues to be informed enough to carry this out. It would be of great benefit to most co-ordinators or directors of small voluntary organisations to have an appraisal of their own performance.

Carla should have allowed more time to sort out the appraisal forms as staff **COMMENT**
are nervous about appraisal interviews even if they have been through one
before. Explaining well in advance and discussing the issues in supervision
sessions can help to allay fears.

Pass on the information to her Management Committee chair so Carla **WHAT CARLA**
can also have an appraisal.   **MIGHT DO**
                                                                      NEXT

SUPERVISION

MANAGING TO ADVISE, Christine Thornton, Federation of Independent Advice Centres, 1998 (forthcoming).

Looks at all aspects of managing an advice centre, including planning and teamwork.

JUST ABOUT MANAGING, Sandy Merritt Adirondack, London Voluntary Services Council, 1998, £12.45.

Looks at all aspects of management in voluntary organisations.

PLANNING TOGETHER: the art of effective teamwork, G. Gawlinski & L. Graessle, NCVO, 1998, £11.95.

Step by step approach to planning as a team.

ASSERTION AND HOW TO TRAIN OURSELVES, Community Education Training Unit, (0422) 35739, 1990.

Training pack on assertion including giving feedback, constructive criticism and dealing with put downs. Ideas for training courses and practical exercises.

TRAINING AND HOW TO ENJOY IT, CETU (see above), 1991, £6.70.

Thirty training exercises designed especially for community groups and voluntary organisations. Themes featured include: groups, meetings, Equal Opportunities, planning and problem solving.

SUPERVISION IN THE HELPING PROFESSIONS, P Hawkins & R Shohet, Open University Press, 1989, £12.99

Excellent resource on supervision within the voluntary sector, offering a very flexible model.

EMPLOYMENT PRACTICE GUIDELINES, Gill Taylor, FIAC, 1993, £5.95 (FIAC members), £9.95 (non-members).

Covers recruitment & selection of staff and equal opportunities policies.

TRAINING: a negotiator's guide, Labour Research Department, 1988, £1.20.

Examines the issues and organisation of training, looking at various types of training and how to train existing employees.

Section 2

PLANNING AND TEAMWORK

Scenarios

7 PLANNING WORKLOADS

How to prioritise

One of *Home Energy*'s funding local authorities announces a new package of 100% grants for aspects of home insulation. As it is a project to use money unspent at the end of the financial year, all the grants have to be authorised by 31 March. It is now 29 October. Simon has been asked, by Bill, an officer who is a helpful regular contact, to publicise the grants to help maximise take-up; he is keen to, particularly in two areas, which have housing in very poor condition, where *Home Energy* has been doing outreach work.

The problem is that the team is fully stretched at the moment, and Robina is due to go on a three-month sabbatical at the end of November — a busy time of year for the centre. Although a locum has been appointed and will start in a fortnight, Simon doesn't expect him to be able to do all that Robina does.

OPTIONS Should Simon:

- Say he is unable to help and give the catalogue of reasons?
- Make the team take on the extra work?

TIPS on planning

- The unexpected always happens. Some contingency time built into the team time 'budget', however difficult to achieve, makes it more possible to cope.
- In voluntary organisations, the need for the work always outstrips the resources available for it. There is therefore always a need to prioritise.

Simon decides to put his dilemma to the team. On a flipchart, he draws **ACTION**
a plan of the next five months, marking out Robina's sabbatical and all
the other holidays he knows about. He notes that as the leave year also
ends at the end of March, some more people will probably need to take
holidays before then. He draws in existing project work, including a
campaign directed at older black residents of one area, which Marcia is
running jointly with Rose, two other targeted take-up campaigns, and
some work Leah is doing to heighten the profile of *Home Energy* itself.

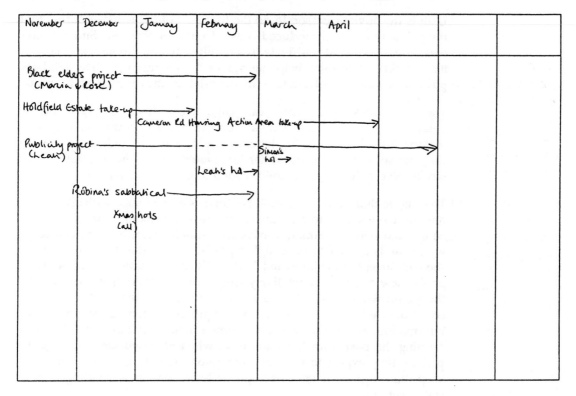

The team agree with Simon that the new insulation grants should be a
high priority. Robina says that the new grants allow them to do more
pro-active work. Jasvinder is less sure, saying the choice of initiative is
scarcely theirs. Carlos suggests that they could advise the council about
how to design and target their publicity material. Although Simon
agrees that this would be a good idea, it does not solve the *Home Energy*
dilemma since their involvement will probably get the attention of more
of the people who really need the grants. He suggests that they identify
the options, and the tasks involved in running a take-up campaign, and
that they then look at how to negotiate with the Council to maximise the
effort they put in.

They identify areas: working with the Council to produce effective leaflets, posters and application forms (which saves them from having to produce them); using regular channels like their newsletter for community groups and builders; leafleting in their target housing areas; speaking at community group meetings and doing extra advice surgeries in their target areas; answering extra telephone queries generated by the work. They estimate that between ten and twenty work days are needed, depending on the response.

Leah is the obvious person to do the first part of the work, ensuring that the publicity material produced is as effective as possible. Simon thinks that Bill will respond positively to tactfully-put suggestions, especially as he has asked for their help; he agrees to set this up. The fall-back position would be for Leah to write material for the centre itself to print.

The team thinks that Leah's campaign about *Home Energy* could be delayed for a while, "especially as you can make sure that the Council's material identifies us in big letters!" Leah is not entirely happy about this, but sees the necessity of her involvement over the next four to six weeks. She is due to go on holiday for a month in January.

They agree that leafleting should be done as a team task, with all of them braving the weather to blitz their two areas. Speaking at meetings is to be divided between Simon, Carlos and Marcia; Marcia's joint campaign with Rose is agreed to have higher priority than other take-up work, so she will do less than Simon and Carlos. The team agrees that as advising on the new scheme is a relatively simple matter, there is no reason why the locum worker cannot do a lot of it; Rose says that in that case she could deal with a lot of the phone enquiries, as long as she has basic information about the scheme. Simon asks Jasvinder to take over opening the post from Rose, (on days when he is working), during the periods they expect to be busy with phone enquiries. They agreed to keep the progress of the campaign under review as a standing item at staff meetings.

OUTCOME As the other campaigns are on-going, it is agreed that until the end of March this campaign should take top priority. Simon agrees that if, as a result, team members find it difficult to take their holidays by then, he will ask the Management Committee to allow people to carry forward more days than are normally allowed. Everyone is pleased that they are doing something positive, and pleased with the way they negotiated the work.

The team agreed the priority of this campaign and made a work plan to **COMMENT**
tackle it in the tight timescale. This was relatively easy as everyone saw its
importance. Some other work is postponed or reduced, and although
everyone will be rather busier than usual, tasks are divided up in a way that
does not place an undue burden on any one person; everyone — including
the administrative and finance workers — is involved.

GENERAL ACTION TIPS

- If one piece of work is given top priority, think through how it will impact on other work.
- Plan methodically by breaking down the work into tasks, putting them into chronological order, and estimating how long they will take.
- In team planning, make sure everyone's interests are treated with consideration.

Talk to Bill again offering to help with the publicity and outlining what **WHAT SIMON**
else they plan to do; make it clear that they have re-scheduled work in **MIGHT DO**
order to help. Think about whether he can build some 'slack' into next **NEXT**
year's work plan. Set up the unusual arrangement for carrying leave
forward with the management committee.

8 MEETINGS

Making staff meetings more productive

Carla's staff meetings don't feel very productive. The agenda seems to get longer each time, and they never get to the end, however much they extend the meetings. Although the team in general works hard, in the meetings people do not seem very involved or to care very much — they are often mucking about — particularly towards the end. It is hard to find the time to have meetings, and sometimes Carla feels the work would get done more efficiently without them.

OPTIONS Should Carla:

- Abolish staff meetings?
- Announce a re-vamp of staff meetings?
- Find out what her staff think the problem is?

TIPS on staff development

- People mucking about in a meeting is a sign that something may be wrong. Carla needs to investigate why that is.

- Carla's sense that the team might be better off without meetings suggests that the meetings have lost or are not serving their purpose.

- Meetings need to be ordered both to get through the necessary business and to allow people to feel comfortable and work effectively.

- Lengthening meeting time to 'finish off' an agenda is unlikely to work if you cannot estimate how long each item will take.

When Carla is not sure what to do, she often talks to her friend Mary. **ACTION**
After work they meet, and Carla shares her frustration. Mary asks what
the meetings are for. Carla says 'to help us plan work together' but
cannot see how the meetings actually help — she could just tell people
what to do in a fraction of the time. Also, there have been several
frivolous agenda items early on recently, which have taken up too much
time. Mary asks how the agendas are set. Carla replies that the 'agenda'
page is always stuck on the noticeboard, so that any member of staff can
put on an item. To this Carla adds anything that she wants to discuss —
she makes a note in her diary as things arise.

"In other words", says Mary, "You don't plan the agendas at all." "I
suppose not", admits Carla, "But we'd have to discuss all those things
anyway." "Why?" asks Mary. She suggests clarifying why *each* item is
on the agenda (is it for discussion, for decision, to allocate tasks, or for
information?) and estimating how long it takes.

Carla realises that discussion at staff meeting is not the most efficient
way to deal with everything, and decides to be more selective. On the
other hand she wants to continue to give her staff access to the agenda.

She puts 'staff meeting structure' at the top of the agenda page for the
next meeting. The discussion is very useful. Everyone has been getting
frustrated because the meetings were so long and chaotic, and because
people are late and take telephone calls, which delays things further.
Carla says that some things might be better dealt with elsewhere, for
instance where what is needed is a conversation between two people, not
the whole team. The team agree that more selection would be
worthwhile.

Alexis offers to take the minutes to allow Carla to concentrate on
chairing; David suggests having a rota for chairing and minutes, so Carla
and Alexis can take full part in discussions. Kwame says it takes him a
while to get into a meeting so he doesn't want to do in-depth discussion
in the first 10 minutes; Carla realises that she wants more time at the end
of meetings to sum up what has been agreed, and to relax together.

The team agree: that meetings will start on time and that no interruptions **OUTCOME**
will be allowed   the answering machine will be switched on; to open
their meeting with a 10–15 minute session where everyone says how they
are doing with their work, shares any concerns they have, or tells one
achievement since the last meeting; that the next item should always be
to plan the agenda for the meeting, starting with the 'agenda page' but
putting the most vital things first and making an estimate of how long
each item will take   so some items can be deferred if necessary.

They agree to use a flipchart for this process, and that minutes should be read out at the end of each meeting to make sure that everyone knows what they are supposed to be doing. They also agree that staff meetings should normally last for two hours, with an extra half hour to be kept free which can be used in emergencies — otherwise they will go off and have lunch together after the meetings.

It is agreed to try David's rota idea, but only after they have had a training session on how to chair and take minutes. David, who has been on a meeting skills course, offers to do this.

COMMENT *Carla and her team have tackled the problem head-on and agreed some concrete changes to improve their meetings. The discussion gives Carla a basis on which to challenge unhelpful behaviour in meetings in the future.*

GENERAL ACTION TIPS

- Agenda planning is crucial to effective meetings.
- Structure the meeting so it has a beginning, a middle and an end.
- Interruptions and lack of punctuality are unacceptable.
- Vary styles of chairing to suit the purpose of different agenda items.

WHAT CARLA MIGHT DO NEXT Keep the meetings' effectiveness under review; attend meeting skills training; read up on how to run effective meetings; experiment with different methods, such as brainstorming, listing pros and cons etc.

Ask an outside consultant to help the team work better together.

9 ENCOURAGING TEAM WORK

Working together more effectively

Following the team meeting described in Scenario 3 on Motivation (page 16), Simon had prepared a brief for a consultant to come and work with the team. At the next meeting Robina says that the team should amend the brief and a team member should interview consultants with Simon. Although a bit surprised, most team members support this view, and Simon agrees to it.

Now the time has come for the first session with the consultant. Rose has borrowed a training room from the Council in an old Victorian House with grounds. Simon is feeling nervous. What will happen? What will team members say about him? Although the consultant was very careful to clarify the objectives of the two days and has sent an outline programme, Simon isn't really sure what to expect.

The first day is very good. Some ground rules are agreed, and the team do several exercises, most of which focus on the work. There is very little disagreement about objectives, and there is a real sense of unity as they debate what work should have the highest priority.

The second day proves more challenging for Simon. It emerges that most team members feel isolated and unsupported a lot of the time. The only person who doesn't say this is Carlos, who doesn't say much at all, despite the efforts of the consultant, Simon and others. Simon is shocked. He feels he has failed as a manager, particularly as he has had no inkling that this is a problem. He gets defensive and points out that it is not surprising, as most people have to work alone a lot of the time.

Should Simon: OPTIONS

- Keep a stiff upper lip and try to ignore it?
- Say what he feels?
- Try to find out more?

> **TIPS on teambuilding**
>
> - Teambuilding draws on the resources of the whole group to strengthen group communication and effectiveness. Each team member is encouraged to take responsibility for her/his own words and actions. This can include raising uncomfortable feelings, as people may say things that have remained unsaid for some time. It can be particularly difficult for managers, who may feel partly responsible for any negative feelings that emerge.
> - Feelings that are expressed can be dealt with, or may change, or their root causes can be addressed. So managers should aim to be as open as they can in the situation. In some cases, such as with a very new and inexperienced team who need a strong leader figure, or where there are not adequate safeguards, openness may not be appropriate.

ACTION The consultant asks Simon how he feels about what has been said. He feels choked, but says that he feels a failure, especially because no one had spoken to him about the problem. Robina says "Crap!" and Leah points out that as he has only been in post nine months and most of them have been feeling this way for much longer, it can't possibly be all his fault. Marcia says that his predecessor, June, would not have been interested. Jasvinder says that because Simon seems so together himself, it can be difficult to tell him about problems — they want to give him 'good news'.

All this makes Simon feel better, but he is still concerned that the team do not seem to find him approachable. He asks for a ground rule that in future people *do* raise problems with him — "I'd rather know", he says. As part of the process the team agree a set of ground rules for how they behave with each other, spelling out a lot of what they do already. The key words, as Rose says, are respect, involvement, honesty and courtesy. The groundrules give any team member a basis for challenging each other on departures from these standards.

OUTCOME The team also agree several measures to reduce their feelings of isolation and to give time to talk about problems. They decide to start their team meetings with a relatively unstructured 'checking in' session where team members say how they are feeling about their work and any issues that concern them; this could lead, by negotiation, to amending the subsequent staff meeting agenda. Simon agrees to give the team more access to setting the staff meeting agenda; everyone wants more frequent supervision — every other month is not enough; it is agreed to accelerate the timetable for Simon's joint working proposals, and to discuss a more radical option — to broaden the job descriptions so that all fieldworkers do some casework and some pro-active work; it is agreed that Rose can delegate some routine updating to be shared by the team as a whole, to free her to shadow a fieldworker for two days a month.

Rose takes advantage of the new groundrules to challenge Carlos on his lack of participation in the discussion. Carlos agrees that he has been pre-occupied with 'personal problems' and will make more effort to involve himself — which he does for the remaining hour.

Team-based work asks all members of a team to share responsibility for their work. Through the two-day exercise Simon's team became thoroughly involved in planning — except Carlos. Teams can only work by consent — no one can be forced to be more involved than s/he wishes. Working in this way also requires maturity and confidence in the team leader, who will generally relinquish some control over how objectives are reached. Simon instinctively prefers to work by consent where possible, so is comfortable with a team-based approach; but he needs to learn how to delegate more effectively. **COMMENT**

GENERAL ACTION TIPS

- Check out that objectives and values are commonly held.
- Discuss and agree team ground rules.
- Encourage each person to take responsibility.
- Challenge departures from the ground rules.

He might suggest scheduling regular review sessions with the consultant, once or twice a year, for the team to consider their work and their working together in more depth than is usually possible in a staff meeting. **WHAT SIMON MIGHT DO NEXT**

10 PRIORITISING WORK WITHIN THE TEAM

Finding a rational way for deciding what is important

Maghira and her team have set aside some time to talk about the centre's priorities. Maghira has made sure that everyone knows they won't be able to put these to the Management Committee yet, but they can develop their own ideas in preparation.

The discussion starts off pretty well as they identify their objectives, but becomes much more difficult as they start to discuss the merits of one area of work against another. Before long it is a shouting match with everyone asserting the superior importance of her own work. Also, Maghira knows the work *they* value most is not necessarily important to the management committee or funders.

OPTIONS Should Maghira:

- Shout louder than everyone and assert *her* view of appropriate priorities?
- Shut everyone up and spell out the realities of their situation?
- End the discussion?

TIPS on prioritising

- Need always outstrips resources. We always need to prioritise.
- Difficulties over conflicting priorities arise when there are no clear criteria for prioritising one piece or area of work over another.
- In these circumstances each person will prioritise on the basis of their personal values and assumptions, and agreement will be impossible.
- It can be particularly difficult in agencies which have a wide range of roles: which are the essential core activities?

Maghira observes that there seems to be no basis for agreement at **ACTION**
present, and calls a break. When the meeting resumes, she suggests that
each person in the team identify the activities which she regards as
crucial, without discussion. At the end of this there is a shorter list of
activities than were previously under discussion, although the list is still
quite long.

Maghira then raises the question of how one piece of work should be
prioritised against another. What should the principles be? Again she
asks each team member to contribute three. The list they come up with
includes:

- If we don't do this, will our funding be withdrawn?
- If we don't do this, will children be put at serious risk?
- Do we have the resources to do this properly?
- Is this effective in taking forward the organisation's objectives?
- Will doing this make things significantly better for our users?
- Will we achieve a significant effect for relatively little effort?
- If we don't do this now, will it be too late later on?
- If we don't do this, will anyone else?

After the list has been compiled, Maghira and the team discuss it, and, by
voting, put the criteria into an agreed order of priority. They also
identify some further criteria which could be used in marginal cases.
This takes the rest of the meeting time they have allocated, so a further
time has to be set for the priorities discussion; but by the end of it
everyone feels much clearer about the basis on which decisions should be
made.

The team didn't agree any order of priorities at this meeting, but did **OUTCOME**
achieve a basis on which to proceed.

Maghira took firm control of the meeting after the break, and imposed a **COMMENT**
*process but did not impose a solution. This was wise, as imposed solutions
are rarely as stable as agreed ones. The team still has some way to go —
and that is before they try to convince a partly unsympathetic Management
Committee.*

GENERAL ACTION TIPS

- In setting priorities, it is important to clarify objectives *and* criteria.

- Some criteria will be principle- or value-based, and some will be pragmatic.

- Don't be discouraged by the first disagreement. Disagreement leads to better quality decisions if a process to resolve it can be agreed.

WHAT MAGHIRA MIGHT DO NEXT   Talk to her staff some more about the key concerns of funders and the issues for the Management Committee; plan a process carefully for the next discussion.

11 DELEGATION AND RESPONSIBILITY

When to relinquish control but retain responsibility

Simon has become aware that he needs to delegate some of his work to team members for two reasons — his very experienced team have become somewhat stale and need new challenges, and he has too much to do — lately he has been working very long hours and as he has been unable to take all his time-off-in-lieu, has lost the hours that he has worked above the 30 hour cut-off point.

Should Simon: **OPTIONS**

- Put things to the team and ask which bits of his job they would like to do?
- Decide what he doesn't want to do and delegate that?
- Identify the different elements of his job first?

TIPS on delegation

- Before delegating, analyse your own job — which things *must* you personally do?
- Do not delegate anything that is central to your role as a manager, or which requires confidentiality.
- Do not delegate anything where the delegated role and boundaries cannot be defined, or where a conflict with organisational values may arise.
- Don't delegate all the work you don't like.
- Having decided what to delegate, think about who could do it, either now or after training.

THINKING   Simon identifies six areas of responsibility in his job: coordination and planning; Management Committee liaison; staff support and supervision, including casework support; managing resources; representing the centre; and field work.

Although Simon could delegate field work, he doesn't think it would be a good idea — his colleagues would not gain any *new* challenges, and he would be cut off from direct involvement in the main work of the centre; the new team working approach means that the team share in the planning, but as manager he feels he must retain overall control of the processes; he manages all the centre's resources, and thinks that he could delegate some of his role in managing the building and looking after petty cash. Rose might be interested in doing that; he represents the centre at a number of meetings and action groups, which is work that the field staff could do; he feels he must continue to be the main liaison person for the Management Committee, but sees ways of involving staff more directly in reporting to it; he sees his staff support and supervision role as central, but thinks that casework support could perhaps be handled more effectively by the group as a whole.

ACTION   At the next team meeting Simon tells the team that he is interested in delegating his role in representing the centre to three regular meetings; he describes what is involved, and asks who would be interested. He also raises the idea of regular casework support sessions where he and the energy advisers would discuss difficult cases together.

He speaks to Rose in her next supervision session about whether she would like to take on more responsibility for the building and for petty cash. She says that normally she would like to, but that because of personal circumstances, at present she does not want to; she might be interested in six or nine months time.

The next day, in her supervision session, Marcia asks to attend a 'Women into Management' course; she adds that she would be interested in any opportunities for experience of management roles. Simon suggests that she take on some responsibility for building management for 12 months. Marcia is not filled with enthusiasm for this, but recognises that the experience may be useful; she offers to do it if she can also 'shadow' Simon as he negotiates the next year's grants and completes the applications. Simon tells Marcia that he sees her as having good management potential, and says he will think some more about what opportunities he can offer her.

Simon successfully delegates some non-essential work to offer colleagues **OUTCOME**
new opportunities, and creates new structures for casework support
which help relieve the pressure on him. The 'shadowing' arrangement
he agrees with Marcia means that at least one other person in the centre
will be familiar with the grant application process, *and* he has managed
to delegate some work he dislikes (building management) to someone to
whom it is useful experience.

Robina has asked for a three-month unpaid leave of absence to research
career and education options, which has been agreed; she will not be
going for four months which allows some time to plan and to appoint a
locum adviser. Simon decides to ask Marcia to work with him through
the whole process of recruiting and selecting the locum, after she has
attended an Equal Opportunities recruitment course. He is also thinking
about asking her to supervise the locum, with his support.

Simon has started well, thinking through what, and to whom, to delegate. **COMMENT**
*He is prepared to give over control, as long as he is confident that the staff
member can fulfil the role; and he is prepared to pay for training, where
necessary.*

GENERAL ACTION TIPS

- Be prepared to relinquish control, while recognising that
  you retain responsibility for any resulting mistakes.
- Communicate clearly the limits of the delegation to
  everyone concerned.
- Review and evaluate the effectiveness of the delegation
  together.

He could clarify the delegation roles and review procedures further; he **WHAT SIMON**
could begin to plan for longer term delegation. He could train and **MIGHT DO**
develop less experienced staff to take over some functions through **NEXT**
delegation.

12 DEALING WITH STAFF NOT GETTING ON TOGETHER

How to deal with personal antagonisms and conflict

Alexis and Kwame just don't get on. They got off to a bad start, and although things got better for a while, recently they have been going downhill. Carla has tried ignoring it, and treating it as a bit of a joke — "Now, now, children" and so on — but neither tactic has worked. They either sulk or are extremely formal with each other. Now they are 'not speaking' and are reduced to communicating through others. Kwame has just asked Fred, their long-standing volunteer, to ask Alexis when she will have his letters ready — in full hearing of Alexis *and* Carla. The atmosphere is dreadful. Carla realises that she cannot let this go on any longer.

OPTIONS Should Carla:

- Bang their heads together — which is what she feels like doing?
- Try to find out what is going on?
- Issue them both with formal warnings?

TIPS on personality clashes

- Even though the behaviour is childish, these are not children. It is important to treat them both with respect, even though their behaviour doesn't merit it.
- It would be inadvisable to issue formal warnings without first trying to find out what the problem is.
- People who work together don't have to like each other. But they do have to treat each other with respect, and they do have to *work* together.
- It is important for the manager to be as clear as possible what change in behaviour they want to see.

Managing People

Carla decides that she will see them both separately first, and then see **ACTION**
them together. She fixes private meetings with them both, stating that
she wishes to discuss the problem caused by the bad feeling between
them.

She prepares a statement to make in both meetings: that their behaviour
to each other falls short of the standards of professional courtesy which
she requires; that the behaviour has become a problem for the project,
which she as the manager has to see resolved; that they do not have to
like each other but they do have to work together. She decides to start,
though, in both cases, by asking them for their version of the problem.

She sees Kwame first. He shrugs his shoulders — "Search me," he says,
"— she just won't talk to me." Carla points out that what *she* saw was
Kwame not talking to Alexis, and asks if it has anything to do with her
work. He says "No, that's fine now. We were getting on quite well, and
at the Christmas outing we had a long chat and I thought we were
getting on really well. But since then she just won't talk to me." Carla
can't get more than this from Kwame, so she makes her statement and
says that she will arrange a meeting between the three of them; in the
meantime she expects Kwame to speak directly and courteously to Alexis
when the work requires it. He agrees.

Then Carla sees Alexis. When she is asked for her view of the problem,
Alexis bursts into tears. "He just thinks I'm beneath him," she says. "I
don't like him." Carla says "Things seemed to change around Christmas.
Did anything happen?" Alexis isn't willing to say very much at first, but
gradually it emerges that she and Kwame were left in the pub after the
others had gone home. They were having a good time and had both had
'a bit more to drink than we should'. Alexis was finding Kwame very
attractive and towards the end of the evening they were kissing each
other.

"I'm so ashamed," says Alexis. "I don't know what came over me. I'm
not like that at all. My husband would be. . . I haven't been able to tell
anyone." Since then she hasn't wanted to be anywhere near Kwame.

Carla lets Alexis talk for a bit longer, and when she has stopped, tells
Alexis her concerns and expectations as a manager. Alexis is surprised
that Carla doesn't seem to regard what happened as being very dreadful
"I've never been unfaithful before," she says. Carla points out that
everyone makes mistakes, and this was quite a small one; Alexis doesn't
have to keep on worrying about it, but can put it behind her. "Do you
think I should tell my husband?" Alexis asks. "Why make another
person unhappy?" asks Carla.

OUTCOME The next day Carla sees Kwame and Alexis together. Kwame says that he finds Alexis attractive and didn't understand why she had changed towards him. "If she doesn't want anything to come of it, that's OK," he says. "But she doesn't have to be so cold to me." Alexis says that she thought Kwame considered her 'loose', but that she feels much less guilty now that she has spoken to someone. She adds that she feels confident that God has forgiven her. They are able to discuss what happened and agree that it was a mistake. The meeting seems to clear the air, and while Kwame and Alexis continue to be somewhat wary of each other, the bad feeling and childish behaviour has gone.

COMMENT *Problems are not always what they seem! Carla decided to investigate the problem first, and the investigation itself resolved the problem behaviour. If it had not done so, or with another kind of problem, Carla would have to spell out what professional standards of behaviour she required, and to make clear to Kwame and Alexis that if they continued to fall below these, the disciplinary procedure would be used. Carla did very well, though she could perhaps have acted sooner.*

Also, sexual relationships between colleagues are rarely straightforward! Attractions are inevitable, but acting on them is risky.

GENERAL ACTION TIPS

- Don't deal only with the obvious. Investigate thoroughly.
- Take informal action to deal with problems before using formal routes.
- Treat people and their feelings with respect, even if they are behaving badly.
- Be clear exactly what standard of behaviour you will accept, and stick to your guns.

WHAT CARLA MIGHT DO NEXT Attend a course on counselling skills for managers.

13 LONG TERM VOLUNTEERS

Volunteer management issues

Health Youth Action has a volunteer, Fred, who has worked with the organisation for years — he was there before Carla joined. Fred used to manage a graphic design department, but became unemployed due to ill-health, and is very dedicated and skilled — he has always produced all the centre's leaflets and promotional literature, working closely with David and Kwame. He has never needed much support from Carla, getting on with his work, pleasant to the staff, reliable.

But things have changed. Fred seems to have less to do and appears less contented; the national organisation's new leaflet unit is now producing high quality material, and the unit has less need to produce its own. At the same time Carla is under pressure from the Management Committee to recruit more volunteers so that the unit can do more work for the same budget. She is rather dubious about this, as it sounds a bit too simple; Carla already has enough to do, and suspects that not all volunteers are as trouble-free as Fred.

Should Carla:

OPTIONS

- Give Fred another 'job'?
- Recruit some more volunteers?
- Find out some more about what she is getting into?

Carla arranges lunch with her friend Mary, who has volunteers working **RESEARCH** for her. Mary has just been on a course about managing volunteers, and is full of enthusiasm. "You have to provide a proper structure," she says, "And you *must* have some idea why they want to work in your organisation." Mary promises to give Carla some of the handouts from the course, and a copy of the draft volunteer policy she is working on for her own agency. She adds that she has given herself a year to get her programme properly sorted out. Carla is now sure that managing volunteers properly is a job in itself. She doesn't even know why *Fred* volunteers, let alone any potential volunteers.

MARY'S HANDOUT

VOLUNTEERS NEED ORGANISATIONS TO:

- Be committed to volunteers and have thought through how they fit in
- Have earmarked resources (volunteers don't come completely free!)
- Have identified one or more clear volunteer jobs
- Advertise and recruit volunteers with those jobs in mind
- Select volunteers who match the jobs
- Induct and train the volunteers so they feel at home and are equipped to do the job
- Tell volunteers who their supervisor is
- Give volunteers adequate support to do the job
- Review things with the volunteer regularly

ACTION   Carla now arranges to have lunch with Fred. She asks him how he got involved. "If I'd known some of this stuff when I was younger, I wouldn't have got so ill so fast", he says. "Plus, designing the leaflets keeps me sharp — I know I can still do it, even if I can only manage two days a week."

Carla talks to him about the improved material coming out of the national organisation. "Making me redundant", he says. Carla is quite sure there are many organisations which need what Fred can do, and says so — but adds that what he does at *Health Youth Action* is much appreciated. Fred is pleased, and reminds her that he particularly wanted to work with *them* because they give health information to young people.

She asks his opinion about setting up a volunteer programme. "There are loads of things volunteers could do", he replies, "but it would have to be set up properly." As he tells her his ideas and they talk, he becomes quite excited at the prospect; Carla remembers that he was also a manager and a brilliant idea hits her: Fred could develop and run the volunteer programme! They agree that he will attend the next staff meeting so that the ideas can be discussed by everyone, before she takes a proposal to the Management Committee.

At the staff meeting, people feel that there are several roles volunteers **OUTCOME**
could fill in the unit, that some unemployed people might like to. It is
agreed Fred and Carla should work together to make a proposal for the
Management Committee, to take things forward over a sensible
timescale; everyone agrees that a policy is needed, and that volunteers
shouldn't be taken on without a proper structure for support and
training.

Carla and Fred managed to turn two problems — dealing with the loss of **COMMENT**
Fred's role, and the pressure from the Management Committee for more
volunteers — into an opportunity. She is also better equipped to deal with
the committee, because she now realises that managing volunteers requires
time, effort and money.

GENERAL ACTION TIPS

- Before recruiting volunteers, an organisation should clarify, at management committee level, why it wants volunteers and how they should be 'employed' and treated.

- Further issues to consider include limitations, of space, money, time, or role; who is to be responsible for supervising and supporting the volunteers; what training paid staff need to work effectively with and alongside volunteers; payment of expenses and other volunteer costs such as training.

- Allow a realistic timetable to develop a programme; planning properly now saves time later.

- Don't be tempted to shortcut the process: there are volunteers with whom a less structured approach will work, but not for any significant number, and the arrangement will be fragile — dependent on the individuals concerned.

With Fred, develop a volunteer policy and a plan for developing the **WHAT CARLA**
volunteer programme over time. She and he could also attend a training **MIGHT DO**
course themselves. **NEXT**

MORE INFORMATION ON:

PLANNING AND TEAMWORK

MANAGING TO ADVISE, Christine Thornton, Federation of Independent Advice Centres, 1998 (forthcoming).

> *Looks at all aspects of managing an advice centre, including planning and teamwork.*

EVALUATION IN THE VOLUNTARY SECTOR, Mog Ball, Forbes Trust, 1988, £4.95

> *Examines all aspects of evaluation for voluntary groups — from the process to the practice of evaluation.*

PLANNING TOGETHER: the art of effective teamwork, G. Gawlinski & L. Graessle, NCVO, 1998, £11.95

> *Step by step approach to planning as a team.*

UNDERSTANDING VOLUNTARY ORGANISATIONS, Charles B. Handy, Penguin Books, 1985 £3.99

> *Looks at basic concepts and the use of their application to create a more effective organisation.*

GETTING ORGANISED, Christine Holloway & Shirley Otto, Bedford Square Press, 1986, £5.95

> *Ideas to improve planning and evaluation in voluntary organisations.*

WHAT A WAY TO RUN A RAILROAD, Charles Landry et al, Comedia, 1985, £2.50.

> *Looks at collectives and management — the ideals, the reality and the way forward.*

JUST ABOUT MANAGING, Sandy Merritt Adirondack, London Voluntary Services Council, 1998, £12.45.

> *Examines monitoring and evaluation in voluntary organisations.*

MANAGING WITHOUT PROFIT, Mike Hudson, Penguin Books in association with DSC, 1995, £9.99

VOLUNTEERS

ESSENTIAL VOLUNTEER MANAGEMENT, S McCurley & R Lynch, Directory of Social Change, 1998, £14.95

WORKING WITH VOLUNTEERS: Support, Lisa Conway, National Centre for Volunteering, 1994, £4.50

Looks at the motivations of volunteers, the kinds of support they need, and the skills needed in order to provide support.

WORKING WITH VOLUNTEERS: Recruitment & selection, David R Smith, National Centre for Volunteering, 1994, £4.50

Looks at how to get the appropriate volunteer for the task, also covering equal opportunities and protection of vulnerable users.

WORKING WITH VOLUNTEERS: Training, Lisa Conway, National Centre for Volunteering, 1994, £4.50

How to design and evaluate a training programme.

ALL EXPENSES PAID?, National Centre for Volunteering, £1.50

Answers a number of questions relating to volunteer expense payments.

PROTECTING VOLUNTEERS, Cressida Wasserman, National Centre for Volunteering, 1996, £2.00.

Offers guidelines for volunteer organisers in statutory and voluntary agencies.

VOLUNTEERS: welfare benefits and taxation, National Centre for Volunteering, £1.00.

Looks at taxation and volunteers expenses, and also regulations for welfare benefits relating to, and possibly affecting, voluntary workers.

KEY ELEMENTS OF GOOD PRACTICE IN WORKING WITH VOLUNTEERS, Wandsworth Volunteer Bureau, 1994, £10.00

A series of information sheets covering all aspects of working with volunteers.

USEFUL ORGANISATION

NATIONAL CENTRE FOR VOLUNTEERING, Carriage Row, 183 Eversholt Street, London NW1 1BU. *Tel:* 0171-388 9888.

Provides books, pamphlets and resources on volunteers and volunteering.

Section 3

DEALING WITH DIFFICULT SITUATIONS

Scenarios

14 HARASSMENT

Dealing with it quickly and sensitively

Maghira is mortified to come into work one Monday and find a handwritten note from Surinder saying that she has to resign immediately and can't even face coming across the doorstep. Maghira racks her brains to think what might have caused this, but can't think of anything.

OPTIONS **Should Maghira:**

- Make time to go to Surinder's home immediately and find out why?
- Ask the rest of the staff if they know of any reason why Surinder isn't in work?
- Leave it for the moment, but write a letter asking for an explanation?

ACTION Maghira goes round to Surinder the same morning and manages to see her on her own. Surinder is very upset and explains eventually that Kamlesh had made a rude suggestion to her on Friday when they were in the office on their own. He had made a few remarks before of a suggestive nature, but she had either brushed them off or ignored them. She hadn't told Maghira because they hadn't seemed important or threatening. Friday was different because they were on their own and he had sidled up behind her and given her a squeeze. When she told him to stop, he had called her a 'stuck up bitch' who was no good to her husband and who needed a lesson in how to behave. He made as if to hit her. Surinder managed to dodge round him and get outside, although Kamlesh was still making strong attempts to get at her and restrain her.

Maghira feels strong emotions wash through her: she is angered and amazed that this could happen, and that she had had no inkling of his behaviour or potential for abusive behaviour. He had seemed all right to her, and had never treated her with less than respect. She feels outraged that a member of her staff has had to go through this experience, and assures Surinder that she will do everything she can to sort out the situation. She asks her to reconsider resignation and gives her leave for one week. Maghira also says she will phone daily to keep her informed of what is going on.

TIPS on dealing with Harassment

- Harassment is not simple to define: it consists of a range of behaviour which is unwanted, uninvited and often repeated and intrusive. It can be part of an expression of power or domination of one group of people over another, perceived as a threat to the dominant group's existence or power.

- Harassment can take a variety of forms from a violent abusive attack to the 'dripping tap' accumulation of intrusions.

- If workers won't make a formal complaint then managers are limited in what they can do.

- Adopt a policy; make sure staff know about it, and encourage staff to complain if the policy is infringed, even if it seems a minor issue.

Maghira asks Surinder to write down her version of events and asks her **ACTION** if she wants to make a formal complaint. Surinder does. Maghira goes back to the office. Kamlesh has not turned up for work either. She phones his home and asks him why he is not there. He does not respond directly. She asks him to come in for a 2.00 pm interview.

She reads up on the discipline and grievance procedure and looks up the Equal Opportunities Commission (EOC) guidelines on how to handle sexual harassment cases.

She decides on her approach, and phones the chair of the Management Committee. She also contacts a member of the Management Committee who she knows has had experience of this through the union, and he agrees to come to the meeting.

She conducts the interview (making sure minutes are taken) with the Management Committee member explaining that Surinder has made a serious allegation and asking Kamlesh for his version of events.

She establishes that they were both there, that Kamlesh did make himself uncomfortable to Surinder and that he called her a 'stuck up bitch'. He doesn't deny it.

She ensures the minutes are taken and signed by both sides and stops the interview. She immediately suspends Kamlesh and tells him to come back with an adviser or union official next week for a formal disciplinary interview.

She finds the grievance proved and follows the disciplinary procedure for gross misconduct on a charge of sexual harassment and attempted violence against a member of staff. She informs the chair of the Management Committee and fixes a date for the disciplinary hearing

She checks with the EOC and the union about procedures to follow and whether an offence of this nature can be followed by immediate dismissal.

She tells Surinder what is going on.

OUTCOME The disciplinary hearing is held one week later, and follows the correct procedures. Kamlesh still seems unrepentant and does not deny the charges. The executive decide to dismiss him unconditionally. They inform him of his right to appeal and go to an industrial tribunal.

Surinder withdraws her resignation and is offered specialist counselling by the Management Committee.

COMMENT *If the case were less clear cut or if Kamlesh had denied that the incident took place, there could have been a lot more convolutions to the scenario. If all staff are made aware of the policy and are encouraged to report minor incidents straight away, there would have been more grounds for Surinder's case had Kamlesh denied it and it became a case of 'his word against hers' — which are always the most difficult cases.*

If there is an element of doubt about the cut off point between disciplinary action and dismissal, always consult an expert before taking final action: your solicitor, the EOC, or the CRE.

Maghira did well; she took immediate and direct action and followed the appropriate guidelines under difficult circumstances, and she supported Surinder well.

WHAT TO DO NEXT Develop a harassment policy and publicise it to all workers.

GENERAL ACTION TIPS

- Adopt definitions

  Write definitions of what constitutes unacceptable behaviour, and what may constitute harassment and discrimination and adopt them as part of a code of conduct or ground rules for the organisation. Make harassment a disciplinary offence. Ground rules which include a 'no-harassment' clause can be used as part of meetings procedure, training courses or for general conduct.

- Publicise

  Publicise these definitions and the consequences of such behaviour to workers, volunteers, Management Committee or Board members, users or clients as appropriate.

- Train workers and volunteers

  Train people in how to handle discriminatory comments or behaviour from users or clients.

- Policy and procedure

  Appropriate managers should be involved in drawing up a specific procedure for dealing with harassment or discrimination. Consider bringing in outsiders trained to deal with such cases.

- Allegations

  Take them seriously. As well as being potentially unlawful, harassment can greatly affect the morale and performance of employees. Don't assume that people making allegations are being over-sensitive.

- Investigation

  The investigation of all grievances of this type must be carried out quickly and properly. The starting point should be the victim's perception of events. If they believe that a certain act was designed to harass them due to their race, sex, sexuality or disability, then that belief must form the basis of the investigation. All other matters should be dealt with separately. The investigation must establish:

  * Was the act in question harassing and causing grievance?

  * Was it racially or sexually motivated or by prejudice against lesbians, gay men or people with disabilities? Would someone in a similar situation but of a different race, sex or sexuality, or physical or mental ability have been treated similarly?

GENERAL ACTION TIPS *continued*

    * *Has the harassment caused a deterioration in the employee's job performance?*

- Counselling employees

  Provide employees with sympathetic counselling.

- Redress

  Take action to redress the injury and discrimination suffered by the victim by preparing a plan of action with them and carrying it out. It could involve for example:

  * *Taking disciplinary action against the perpetrator.*

  * *Changing reporting or working relationships.*

  * *Relocating the harasser, but with no material advantage.*

  * *Maintaining a record of all incidents for future analysis.*

  Prepare an annual report of all grievances for review of senior staff or equal opportunities committee.

  Deal promptly with racist or other offensive graffiti regardless of whether a complaint is made about them.

- Review

  Monitor and review the procedures and nature of the complaints.

GRIEVANCE PROCEDURE The CRE recommends that the following steps are taken because of the sensitivity of complaints of discrimination:

Informal stage

- Tell the employee that they can be represented by their shop steward, employee representative or an employee of their choice.
- Allow for an initial informal approach which is not recorded in the complainant's personnel file unless they wish to pursue the matter further.
- It is very important to allow the person to have access to a sympathetic person in identifying and resolving problems.

Formal Stage

- If the complaint cannot be resolved informally, then ensure as far as possible, that the grievance is investigated by someone independent of the department to which the grievance relates, who has been trained to understand how racial discrimination (or other discrimination) and harassment take place and the hurt it can cause.

- Make it clear that discrimination and harassment are disciplinary offences, the penalty for which may include dismissal.

- Communicate the outcome of the grievance, including any disciplinary action taken against the offender, to the complainant with a written undertaking that they will not be victimised or suffer any other detriment.

- Inform employees of their legal right to apply to an industrial tribunal for a decision on the matter (within three months of the original incident) in the case of race, sex or harassment on the grounds of political belief or religion in Northern Ireland.

Counselling

- Offer counselling to employees who believe that they have suffered unfair treatment, harassment or victimisation.

The grievance and disciplinary procedures that are developed must include placing people on the grievance and disciplinary panel who have experience of dealing with racial, sexual or heterosexual harassment cases. If necessary get an outside person to attend the panel who has got the experience. The panel must be trained to deal sensitively with the issues and to have worked out any attitudes they may have towards harassment before becoming panel members.

There should, as a matter of course, be at least one woman on the panel, or black and ethnic minority person, lesbian or gay person according to who has complained of harassment. Representatives may have to challenge any prejudices that arise during the process of dealing with the case as well as the incident itself. The complainant must have a supporter with them at any stage of the grievance procedure to help in putting the case if necessary.

Once the grievance has been settled, and if the case has legitimacy then the disciplinary procedure should be invoked against the harasser. This may result in the procedure for gross misconduct being used, which might result in suspension or dismissal. Action must also be taken to redress the injury to the complainant. If anyone is to be moved to another job within the organisation then it should be the harasser who moves and they should never gain in grade or financially out of a move.

Suggestions for employees' action in cases of harassment

If a person is being harassed the following recommendations of the EOC in the case of sexual harassment may be helpful in providing a guideline for action.

- The harasser should be told to desist from further unacceptable conduct.

- The management should be informed immediately. Make use of the grievance procedure where appropriate.

- The person being harassed should keep a diary of incidents so that these can be recalled accurately at an organisational enquiry or any subsequent industrial tribunal.

- The person affected should confide in a colleague and inform the union or employee representative and ask for support. It may be that other people have suffered similar harassment.

- Advice should be sought from the Equal Opportunities Commission, the Commission for Racial Equality, or the Lesbian And Gay Employment Rights project as appropriate.

- Indecent assault should be reported to the police.

15 WORKERS WITH AIDS OR HIV

Taking an informed view

Jasvinder requests a meeting with Simon one Monday morning and looks very nervous about it. Simon agrees to see him straight away, and they go into one of the quiet interview rooms. Jasvinder says that what he has to say must be kept confidential to him and Simon at all costs. He is prepared for the meeting and points out the duty in the contract to keep matters confidential between employer and employee. Simon points out that he is not the employer technically (the Management Committee are in law) — but Jasvinder insists on the basis that Simon is their delegated representative.

Simon is mystified but agreed reluctantly at first to what Jasvinder requests, with the proviso that it doesn't involve any issue about criminal actions. Jasvinder assures him that it doesn't, and he further insists that no one must be told, not even the chair of the Management Committee. Simon thinks further and agrees with the same provision, that by keeping the matter confidential he is not endangering other staff or the reputation of the organisation.

Jasvinder says that's fine from his point of view. He then discloses that he has HIV. He found out four months ago and has been attending a support group ever since. He is not ill and is not likely to be ill for some time. He felt he ought to tell Simon in case he found out somehow from other people. But he is absolute in his determination that no one else should know.

Should Simon:

OPTIONS

- Refuse immediately to agree to the confidentiality issue?
- Agree and keep completely silent on the matter?
- Review the health and safety procedures and inform himself more of the issues and any dangers for other staff before agreeing to keep it confidential?

TIPS on employment of people with HIV/AIDS

- The contract of employment has an implied duty of trust and confidence and includes a duty on both employer and employee not to disclose confidential information obtained in the course of employment.

Any AIDS policy should follow these principles:

- Since the infection risk is negligible at work there is no justification for anyone to discriminate on the grounds of HIV or AIDS.

- Individuals who know they are infected have no obligation to tell anyone but if they do disclose it then they should be assured of confidentiality.

- People with AIDS should be treated no differently from anyone else suffering from a life-threatening non-contagious illness.

- No one should be told unless absolutely necessary and then only with written consent of the person with HIV.

- Breaking the confidentiality should be considered a serious disciplinary offence.

ACTION   Simon agrees to keep confidentiality while he finds out about any risks to other staff. Jasvinder assures him that there aren't any, but Simon feels out of date on the matter, and needs to reassure himself.

OUTCOME   Simon does some checking up on the transmission of HIV and find that the likelihood of it being passed on at work is just about nil. He thinks about Jasvinder and what he risked in telling him and decides that he is a brave and honest person to take the risk and tells him so. Simon says that in future he will be reviewing the health and safety policy to ensure that it is of benefit to all staff, and he will look over the procedures for long term illness to make sure that the best and most realistic provisions for Jasvinder and *Home Energy* will be in the contract, should the issue arise for Jasvinder or any other staff member.

COMMENT   *Simon has coped well with a very difficult managerial issue. The hardest part has been to not tell anyone — not even the chair of the Management Committee or his live-in partner. He struggled with that and eventually realised that he owed it to Jasvinder not to break confidentiality with the attendant risks to him.*

GENERAL ACTION TIPS

- People infected with HIV can remain healthy for years (often up to ten or more) before AIDS develops and can work and live quite normally during that period.

- HIV is not spread through ordinary work or social contact; not by touch, by water, by air or coughing or sneezing.

- There has been no case where a person sharing a house with a person infected with HIV has been infected by sharing food utensils or domestic appliances.

- Government guidelines state that HIV infection alone does not affect people's ability to do their jobs until they develop illnesses that make them unfit. If they later become ill they should be treated as anyone else with a life threatening illness. Only if their illness affects their ability to do their job should their employer seek medical advice.

- Dealing with long-term illness is difficult in small organisations. However the procedures used should be just the same for People with AIDS or HIV.

- Include harassment on grounds of people having HIV or AIDS as part of the disciplinary and grievance procedures.

- Make sure the health and safety policy is up to date, and that a risk assessment is carried out as this benefits all staff not just those with AIDS or HIV.

WHAT SIMON MIGHT DO NEXT

He might inform himself more about AIDS and HIV and how the virus is spread. He needs to be very clear about the confidentiality aspect of the case. Jasvinder needs his support now and to be reassured that no-one will find out, as the consequences could be catastrophic for him. He will also spend time developing a policy on AIDS and employment.

16 SMOKING POLICY

Even passive smoking is injurious to health

Simon receives a complaint from Leah about the smoking in the office. Marcia and Rose both smoke at their desks even though the 'official' smoking place is in the kitchen. Leah says it is making her ill and aggravating her asthma. She wants Simon to do something about it and enforce the ground rules this time. Previous attempts to get a collective agreed view on smoking have lasted about one week.

OPTIONS Should Simon:

- Try the same route again and say all smoking outside or in the kitchen, with no discussion?
- Make everyone clear about the law and passive smoking and negotiate with the two smokers an acceptable solution for all?
- Ignore Leah's comments as whingeing?

TIPS on a smoking policy

- Under the Workplace Health and Safety Regulations, employers are obliged to provide separate rest areas for smoking and no-smoking or to ban smoking in rest areas Employees do not have a 'contractual right to smoke'.

- An employee could bring a claim for negligence against an employer if the employer has failed to respond to the harmful effects of smoking in the workplace.

- A tribunal has recognised the harmful effects of passive smoking, which adds impetus for employers to recognise and safeguard the interests of non smokers.

- If the employer wishes to introduce a new rule on no-smoking, the employees should be consulted first.

Simon brushes up on his health and safety legislation. He realises that **PLANNING** something has to be done that will stick as a policy. He decides that the best tools he has are information and persuasion.

He sees Marcia and Rose separately to point out that he has decided that **ACTION** the smoking policy has to be changed, made more forceful and implemented. He explains the legal reasons behind this and asks for their reactions.

He then drafts a smoking policy and presents it at the next staff meeting. This has headings of:

- What the policy is
- Reasons why they are introducing it (health and safety)
- Clear limits on where people can smoke
- That this is enforceable through the disciplinary and grievance procedure
- That this now forms part of the contract of employment

There is a heated discussion at the meeting — Leah walks out at one **OUTCOME** point. Simon suspends the meeting to discuss the difficulty with her in private and comfort her. He goes back into the meeting and reminds everyone that there are ground rules for how meetings are conducted, and asks people take a moment to calm down and read through them.

He brings the meeting to order and conducts the rest of the discussion to formal ground rules: no interruptions; giving feedback in a calm way; asking for information carefully; not making assumptions about others' motivation or feelings. Staying calm throughout, he manages to gain all staff's agreement to the new policy by ensuring that all people have their opinion heard and are allowed to vent their feelings.

Simon acted carefully to bring about an agreed conclusion. He treated the **COMMENT** *issue more seriously than before and made sure that all sides were heard. He is hopeful this time that the policy will stick. As it is now a formal part of the contract, it has the backing of the discipline and grievance procedure, to be used in extreme cases of non-co-operation.*

GENERAL ACTION TIPS

- More workplaces are adopting no-smoking premises rules after consultation with staff and giving employees time to give up the habit — for example up to four months. They often provide counselling and other inducements to giving up.

- It is lawful for employers to advertise for and recruit non-smokers and to incorporate a non-smoking term in the contract of employment.

- Simon will have to be vigilant and challenge any infringements as soon as they happen, now that the smoking policy has been made more formal.

- If the staff hadn't managed to agree, Simon would be in a difficult position, because technically Leah has grounds to go to an industrial tribunal if the workplace does not have no-smoking workrooms and rest areas. Simon would have had to be stronger about enforcing it under health and safety grounds.

WHAT SIMON MIGHT DO NEXT Brush up on his health and safety law and reflect that *Home Energy* could have been taken to a tribunal by Leah.

17 ABSENTEEISM

Finding out what the real problem is

Maghira has discovered from Kamlesh that Shakti has phoned in yet again to say she will not be in for work as she has a back problem. Shakti has taken four periods of three days off work in the last two months. Each time she has produced the self-certification form, and cited a different problem each time.

Maghira sighs and thinks that she really has to bite the bullet. She must have a difficult conversation with Shakti on her return. Shakti had been working fine until two months ago when something happened in her personal life — but no one knows what, and she has not talked about it formally in supervision sessions.

Maghira sorts out with Pratibha the tangle of Shakti's meetings and appointments, and divides up the work among the group. Everyone is very fed up.

Should Maghira:

OPTIONS

- Write to Shakti and say she wants to have a formal talk as soon as she returns to work?
- Leave it informal, but pull her in when she comes back?
- Do nothing?

When Shakti comes back to work on Wednesday Maghira decides to take her aside in the lunch hour for a serious talk. Maghira prepares for the meeting and decides to take a low key approach to try and find out the underlying causes in a careful way first of all. She will then decide on her course of action after hearing what Shakti has to say. **PLANNING**

When Maghira sees Shakti she tries to find out the reasons behind the illnesses and asks if she has been to her GP and what he has to say. Shakti agrees that her health is not good at the moment but that she can't see what she can do about it. **ACTION**

> **TIPS on absenteeism**
>
> - Absenteeism of this sort is often not simple to sort out. It may be the result of difficulties at home or motivational issues which are contributing to or exacerbating genuine health problems.
> - It is important to deal with and find out the underlying causes. Otherwise the organisation keeps losing time and energy that it can ill afford and the rest of the staff have to take the burden of the employee's absence, which can lead to resentment.
> - If there are frequent short absences that the employee has self-certificated but they have not been to a doctor, you can suggest that they go to their GP for advice.

Shakti says she is under a lot of pressure but she won't open up. Maghira decides not to push her too hard, but makes it clear that she expects her to visit the GP and see what he can do for her.

After another two months have gone by, Shakti is still taking time off almost one day each week. Maghira decides to have another go at finding out what is wrong.

She interviews Shakti more formally this time and says that if her rate of sick leave doesn't improve then Maghira will have to take further steps to investigate the problem as the organisation can't cope with the level of absence and the extra workload this causes for the others. If Shakti has a genuine long-term health difficulty, then they need to know about it so they can take the right action.

Shakti then tells Maghira that it isn't so much her health as her mother-in-law, who has arrived on a long-term stay and has health problems herself. She thinks that Shakti is neglecting her children by going out to work and causes her lots of practical difficulties. Far from helping out, she even hinders the other members of her family who had been helping with childcare.

Maghira is understanding and offers her some advice that she must talk seriously to her husband to form a joint approach to her mother-in-law to set some boundaries and make her realise that Shakti wants to live a different life and her husband agrees. Shakti agrees to try.

GENERAL ACTION TIPS

- If continual absences are causing problems in the workplace, the employer can remind the employee that they can't go on indefinitely and can set a timetable for improvements or minimisation of the absences.
- After the fourth period of absence the employee can be asked to attend a medical examination by the DSS for SSP purposes.
- If the frequency of absence is still not reduced, then the procedure for assessing long-term sickness can be used. This may result in dismissal for 'capability' or 'some other substantial reason' if not enough improvement is made. If the dismissal is on the grounds of not enough skill or the aptitude of the worker, the employer would have to show that they gave clear standards expected, warnings, and a timetable for improvements that was not met.
- This may seem harsh, but the organisation may no longer be able to carry an employee who is continually very ill.

OUTCOME

Shakti is still taking the odd day off but is now taking it as unpaid leave up to five days per year to cope with her family difficulties by temporary agreement with Maghira.

Maghira has decided in future that she will talk formally to anyone who takes even one day off sick to find out what is going wrong from the start. She feels she let this problem slide for too long before tackling it.

COMMENT

In long-term or regular small periods of sickness it can be very difficult to sort out what the real issue is behind the absence. On the one hand, as employers you want to ensure the best service for your clients and have the staff on the job as near 100% of the time as possible; on the other hand, workers are people as well with real difficulties that may need help in sorting out. As a general rule always try and find out what the true picture is before leaping to conclusions and try and reach a compromise position which gives the best for the worker and the organisation.

WHAT TO DO NEXT

Make sure that she keeps to her resolution to monitor sick leave at an early stage.

18 LONG-TERM SICKNESS

Dealing with long periods of absence

David has been taking an increasing amount of time off lately. He has had two periods of two weeks off in the last three months and is looking very unwell. His rate of work has slowed right down, and he can't seem to cope with the usual demands of the job. He struggles in to work, but doesn't seem well. Carla is concerned about his health and the effect it is having on the work for the other staff. The Unit is so small that one person under par is a serious burden.

OPTIONS Should Carla:

- Ask David what is the matter straight out?
- Get an independent assessment of his health?
- Leave it another month and see if he gets better?

TIPS on absence

- It makes sense to deal with these issues as soon as possible as the longer it goes on the more serious it can become (and the effects on the organisation can mount).

- It is vital to find out the true medical state of workers before taking any further action or deciding on a course of assessment.

ACTION Carla decides to see David straight away to ask him what is the matter or what he has done so far deal with the problem. She feels anxious in case he is going to be seriously ill for a long time and is impatient to get things sorted out.

David is both shocked and relieved to be able to talk to Carla about it. He says that he feels weak and lethargic most of the time — but not quite ill enough to stay off work.

Carla asks if there have been any changes in home circumstances that might result in stress levels increasing. He says no. She then asks what his GP thinks about the problem. David shuffles in his chair and says that after the last bout of illness he didn't feel like going back to his GP as he was very unsympathetic to his illness and virtually suggested he was malingering.

Carla is sympathetic, and being a health promotion worker she knows what to suggest: that he try another GP in the same practice and ask for blood tests. She gives him two weeks to sort out a medical report, and says that he should come straight to her if they still won't do it.

David finds the results of his tests show that he has glandular fever. He phones from home to say that he will be off for three to six months and needs bed rest. He sounds relieved that he now knows what the problem is.

OUTCOME

Carla at least knows what is going on, but now has further problems: how to handle David's absence for an indeterminate period. She looks up the contract and sees that they have a generous sick pay scheme. After two years of service David will be eligible for 2 months on full pay and 2 months on half pay less any SSP contributions. Unfortunately, *Health Youth Action* do not have large reserves — not large enough to pay for David's sick pay and for a locum worker to take over his duties in his absence.

David will be eligible for SSP for 28 weeks. As *Health Youth Action's* National Insurance bill is less than £20,000, they will be able to claim back 80% of the money paid as SSP by deducting it from the NI bill.

Carla also remembers that all the HPUs around the country have paid into a health insurance scheme taken out by the national office. She checks on the scheme and finds that they will be able to claim back most of the sick pay for David up to six months incapacity. Carla heaves a sigh of relief.

This means that they can employ a locum for four months at least, and up to six months if David is still not well.

COMMENT

It is almost always worth having some sort of private sickness insurance scheme for workers so that their absences do not break the back of the organisation, which may not have any reserves to cover sick pay for long periods and pay a locum wage. Alternatively you will have to draw on your reserves or do some additional fundraising.

GENERAL ACTION TIPS

Small organisations are often in a severe quandary when staff become ill over long periods. It is necessary to try and find a reasonable balance between good employment practice and the needs of the organisation. These are some ideas that small organisations could consider:

- Changes in hours or changes in duties to something lighter when recovering from an illness.

- Being allowed to work from home for a time.

- Being able to take breaks during the day at work where people can lie down or rest in a quiet room.

- Negotiate a mutually agreed time for keeping the job open if people have to take longer off work than their sick leave.

- Alter the working environment to cope with a long-term disability.

- In the last resort, it is legally fair to dismiss an employee on the grounds of ill health, if a proper procedure is followed.

WHAT CARLA MIGHT DO NEXT

Look up the law on fixed-term contracts and work out how to get a locum.

Make sure that the insurance premium is paid on time.

19 INAPPROPRIATE USE OF LANGUAGE

It's much more important than 'political correctness'!

Carla and the rest of the staff are in a *Health Youth Action* staff meeting. Carla is outlining some tentative ideas she has for a promotion campaign in local schools and youth clubs on HIV/AIDS issues for teenagers. Alexis looks up from her minutes and appears slightly shocked. "Surely there's none of them round here", she says. "None of whom?" replies Carla. "Those poor suffering people — those AIDS victims."

Now it is Carla's turn to be shocked at Alexis' ignorance of basic health facts which affect the local area. She is also disquieted by her use of the phrase 'AIDS victims'. Carla knows that Alexis has not been working for HYA for very long, but she can't have helped but hear discussions that have gone on in the office and over the phone advice line. It is a matter of policy that people with AIDS should be referred to by just that term 'People with AIDS', rather than as AIDS sufferers or AIDS victims.

Carla feels frustrated and impatient that she is going to have to spend time with Alexis on the issues when she has little enough time to spend on her other work.

Should Carla: OPTIONS

- Have it out with Alexis then and there in the meeting?
- Stop the meeting for a coffee break and explain in the break why what she said was inappropriate?
- Wait until after the meeting and go over the issue with her?

Carla takes Alexis aside during the break and says that she would like to **ACTION** explain a few things to her. She asks how much Alexis knows about HIV and AIDS; Alexis blushes and says that she didn't think that married Christian women needed to know about things like that.

Carla dispels some myths about the transmission of HIV and who is affected by the virus. They then spend some ten minutes discussing the

---

TIPS on use of language

- It is not appropriate to wait or to do it in front of the other staff. If Alexis is to hear what Carla is saying to her she needs quiet and not to feel that she is 'under the spotlight'.

- However impatient Carla feels, it is worth getting her priorities straight: not everyone has the same attitudes or knowledge about issues of appropriate language. Alexis needs to be informed first, and then she should be not only aware of the issues but capable of being an ambassador for good practice from the organisation.

- Equal opportunities should cover not only the written policies of the organisation, but also the way the work is carried out including the language people use.

- All staff should be encouraged to challenge language that breaches the equal opportunities policy, and may need training in how to make such challenges sensitively.

---

preferred use of the term 'People with AIDS or HIV'. Carla explains that it comes from discussions within the movement of people with AIDS themselves deciding how they would like to be referred to and that it enhances the dignity and respect for the people concerned, rather than being called AIDS victims or AIDS sufferers.

Alexis feels taken aback by all this information, but agrees that Carla has handled it in a sensitive way and that she now understands much better what the team are trying to do on the issue. She agrees to take away one of the Health Education Council booklets and read through it.

OUTCOME The staff meeting resumes and everyone feels more able to take part in the debate in the knowledge that all staff can now respect the reasons for the campaign and the most appropriate language to use.

COMMENT *It is important to encourage people to discuss 'difficult' or sensitive issues rather than sweep them under the carpet and pretend they don't exist. By taking Alexis' lack of knowledge seriously Carla showed to her and the rest of the staff that she is prepared to take the time to explain issues (and listen to open and honest debate carried out) in the spirit of understanding rather than baiting or cynicism. She gave her good feedback in a way in which she was able to hear it.*

GENERAL ACTION TIPS

Ideas for what might go in a policy on use of language:

- Use 'black and minority ethnic people' or 'black people', not 'coloured people'.

- Allow people to self-define the group to whom they feel they belong (e.g. African Caribbean, Somali, Trinidadian).

- Use non-gender-specific language and references, e.g. 'All candidates for interview will be told how *they* have performed' rather than 's/he' or just 'he'.

- Don't make generalisations about groups of people (e.g. stereotyping people with mental health difficulties or people with disabilities).

- Use language and terms which keep in mind and enhance the dignity and respect of the people concerned (e.g. 'People with AIDS' not 'AIDS sufferers' or 'AIDS Victims', 'People with Learning Difficulties' not 'the mentally handicapped').

- Don't use jargon.

Discuss and make available ground rules that include use of language, and display them in a more obvious place.

WHAT CARLA MIGHT DO NEXT

Make sure the induction pack is expanded to cover these issues and what is expected of new staff when answering the phone or talking to people face to face.

Encourage staff to discuss issues of language rather than feel embarrassed

Think about getting some further training for staff on making challenges.

20 PERSONAL USE OF RESOURCES

Setting the boundaries

Maghira has found out by accident that Pratibha has been using the photocopier to do copying for the local playgroup that she chairs. Maghira went along to do some copying herself and found a pile of playgroup minutes. Shakti said that they were Pratibha's and that she was doing some copying late last night. Maghira was initially irritated and then increasingly anxious about what she had found out. Was Pratibha paying for all this? When had she been doing it? — on work time?

OPTIONS Should Maghira:

- Bring it up at the next staff meeting in front of all the staff?
- Talk to Pratibha in private next time she sees her?
- Make a point of finding out as soon as possible through a formal meeting with Pratibha just exactly what has been going on?

TIPS on personal use of resources

- Personal use of resources is a difficult area, as each organisation generally has slightly different custom and practice about copying, pens, paper, phone calls, etc. But unauthorised or continuous use of office resources is tantamount to theft.

- In this case, where Maghira suspects and has now heard it from another member of staff, the matter must be investigated and stopped to prevent gossip, bad feeling, or lack of trust in the staff person concerned.

- Prompt action is the best approach.

- Decide how serious the offence is and treat accordingly: from providing information about rules to formal disciplinary procedure and finally instant dismissal.

Maghira decides to find Pratibha as soon as she can, as the issue is **PLANNING** distracting her from her work. She stops herself acting in anger and sits down to work out what she wants to know: how much copying has she been doing? Has she been paying for it through petty cash? If so who did she set the system up with? When has she been doing this work using the office's facilities?

She realises that Pratibha may have perfectly good explanations and so tries to calm herself and listen to what she has to say before making assumptions about her actions.

Maghira says that she wants to see Pratibha after lunch for half an hour **ACTION** in her office. She tells her what the issue is and asks her the questions outlined above. Pratibha can't really see what all the fuss is about. She didn't see the need to check it out with anyone. She was not using work time but her own time on work premises and the facilities are there to be used aren't they ?

She offered to pay 3p per copy to Kamlesh, who seemed to think that was all right. He put it down in the petty cash accounts as miscellaneous income. Neither of them had seen the need to check it with Maghira, as it seemed too much trouble about nothing.

Maghira is a bit flabbergasted both by her insouciance and her lack of respect for Maghira's authority. She begins to wonder what else Pratibha has been up to without checking through her about policy.

Maghira's background is in local government, where authority is more clear cut than in community groups and where she is used to being consulted on most of the work the staff do. Pratibha's background is in a local women's campaigning group, where there were very different attitudes to use of resources and time spent on work/non-work issues was more blurred.

Maghira accepts that Pratibha was not really intending to defraud the **OUTCOME** organisation; she was just applying different principles that had operated in her last workplace where attitudes were more casual.

She challenges Pratibha to accept that she expects that issues like this should be checked with her first. Maghira makes it plain that she is concerned about boundaries for decision making in the organisation and that this has shown her that she needs to be clearer about her authority and what she expects of the rest of the staff in terms of information sharing and how much autonomy staff have.

Maghira however makes it clear both to Pratibha, Kamlesh and the rest of the staff that whatever has been going on regarding use of resources she thinks this is unacceptably casual and decides to write down what she does think is OK for discussion and agreement.

COMMENT *Maghira has dealt with an issue that needed clarifying. She has also made a wider point about her authority which she felt was not being sufficiently respected in the organisation.*

GENERAL ACTION TIPS

- Personal use of resources is one end of the spectrum working up to theft and dishonesty. Pro-active measures can help prevent the situation getting out of hand.

- Establish clear policies and procedures on what is acceptable and what isn't. Discuss the limits to action with staff and find acceptable boundaries.

- Raise staff awareness at induction training on the organisation's attitudes to resources/perks.

- Review opportunities to reduce dishonesty: less access to the stamps, petty cash etc.

- Dishonesty or theft are sacking offences if the employer has reasonable grounds for the belief that the employee was dishonest and has carried out an investigation.

- Follow the procedures for discipline and grievance for minor infringements but go straight to the procedure for dismissal for dishonesty or theft.

WHAT MAGHIRA MIGHT DO NEXT Write a clear guide for the induction pack on what is acceptable and what is not as part of work time. Especially in small voluntary organisations they sometimes do get used as a bit of a community resource by the people working in them if they are on local committees. It is up to the Management Committee to decide how acceptable this is, and what the boundaries are for using resources. For some organisations, it may be seen as part of the work to offer support to other local groups. For others, involvement in the community may be encouraged as a staff development activity and they may wish to support staff in this through making ancillary office resources available.

21 ALCOHOL ABUSE

Drinking is not just a problem for the drinker

Simon is becoming increasingly concerned about one of the energy advisers, Carlos. Simon knows that Carlos has some difficulties at home, his wife is unhappy and one of his children has been in and out of hospital lately.

Simon has suspected for a couple of months that Carlos is drinking at lunchtime, and this practice is gradually increasing. He often comes into work with a headache as well. Up until now his work has not been affected; but now he is not coping well with his advice sessions. Simon has had some concrete feedback from a regular client that Carlos was impatient and didn't seem to care about the question she was seeking advice on.

Carlos has not said anything formally during his supervision sessions about being under undue stress, and Simon has only picked up his personal situation as part of general conversation at work. The situation is coming to a head and Simon resolves to tackle it this week, but he is unsure how to do it effectively.

Should Simon: **OPTIONS**

- Raise the complaint about his work as part of a formal supervision session that is planned for next week and see if Carlos discloses any personal problems?
- Tell Carlos he wants to see him for a quiet chat sometime today?
- Tell Carlos he'd like to se him at 11.00 am to discuss some feedback he has had about his work?

Simon plans his meeting with Carlos. He writes down the points he **PLANNING** wants to make in the meeting and plans how to open the interview to try and get Carlos to talk. He doesn't want to get him straight onto the defensive.

TIPS on dealing with alcohol abuse

- If you receive a negative comment about someone's work or performance from a third party, check out the situation or event from the worker concerned first.

- Deal with any suspected drug or alcohol abuse straight away; don't wait another week.

- Health and safety legislation makes you liable for your employees' actions — if they should cause an accident while drunk on your premises, you would be liable.

Simon: checks the legal position; checks the discipline and grievance procedure; lists the complaints from the client; and thinks about the outcomes he wants:

- — to probe about the actual complaint

- — to ask why this has happened

- — to obtain better service delivery in future

- — to mention the drinking and relation to poor performance

- — to set clear targets and deadlines for future performance

He plans how to handle the meeting: he will present the issue neutrally, ask Carlos' version and reasons, and they will decide together on short-term and long-term action as a result.

ACTION At the meeting Simon stays calm and goes through the complaint. Carlos looks increasingly uncomfortable, and admits that he made a mistake. Simon presses the point and comments that he has seemed preoccupied lately. Carlos under pressure talks about his difficulties at home. Simon is understanding, but then says that he doesn't think the way to solve them is by drinking. They go on to discuss the legal implications of Carlos' drinking and how Simon can't let the situation carry on as it is.

Carlos admits how much he has been drinking each lunchtime (3 pints) and says that he often drinks beer and spirits each evening too.

Simon then goes on to talk about what he expects from every employee in terms of alcohol use. He sets some clear guidelines for drinking and says he expects Carlos to get outside help to deal with his marital and drink problems. Simon points out clearly that if this schedule is not kept,

Carlos will receive a formal written warning and only one more chance to improve before he is threatened with dismissal.

The contract they come up with is as follows:

- Carlos must not drink alcohol at lunchtimes when he is at work.
- Carlos must seek counselling on his drinking problems and any other problems that may be affecting his work. Simon suggests two different agencies to try.
- Carlos must not come into work so incapacitated that his work is poor.
- They agree that this programme will be reviewed weekly for a month and then a further review meeting will be set.
- They agree that at this stage this will remain confidential between Carlos, Simon and the chair of the Management Committee.
- However, Simon has taken notes of the meeting and asks Carlos to date and sign that he agrees with them as a formal written record of the meeting. This will be needed if any further action has to be taken at a later stage.

Simon handled the meeting well and went on to set clear guidelines for **COMMENT**
action and review dates so that he knows he has clear guidance for any future problems with Miguel's work performance and drinking.

GENERAL ACTION TIPS

- Plan for difficult meetings. Then you can concentrate on the words and interpersonal relationship in the meeting rather than the shape or plan of the meeting.
- Check your legal position and disciplinary and grievance procedure so that you have all the correct facts at your fingertips.

Make sure he knows what to do if Carlos fails to keep to his targets.   **WHAT SIMON**
MIGHT DO
Draft an alcohol abuse policy.   **NEXT**

22 DEALING WITH PERSONAL STRESS

What to do when everything gets too much for you

Maghira is feeling the strain. She has been in her job for five years under constant pressure, with conflicting demands and resources wholly inadequate to the scale of the problem. She has recently had to deal with a major staff problem which resulted in someone being sacked, and is now facing the fallout — a whisper campaign in the community conducted by the supporters of the sacked man — one or two of whom are on the Management Committee. Another stress is the unpredictability of clients' demands. She is totally committed to the centre, and works long hours, often arriving home too tired to pay much attention to her partner or grown-up daughter, Felin, who is training in massage. Felin says it is ironic that Maghira runs a family centre when she has so little time for her own family.

Maghira has noticed that recently she is being irritable at work as well as at home, though only with the staff, not her clients; with the clients she sometimes feels she has nothing more to give; she often feels tired and depressed. She has been to her doctor about recurrent stomach pains; ulcers are suspected and the doctor says she must work less; he suggests that she take a break from her responsibilities and do some training in relaxation.

OPTIONS **Should Maghira:**

- Resign?
- Get on with the job, at least till the current crisis is past?
- Ask Felin for a massage?
- Take her doctor's advice?

ACTION Maghira knows she has to do something. She books a week's holiday. She doesn't want to do relaxation training, but does book a two-day stress management course which she had noticed was coming up soon. Felin is always offering to massage her, as she needs to practise, and Maghira resolves to take up the offer at least once a week.

TIPS on stress management

- Physical and emotional signs of stress should be taken seriously: the problem needs to be tackled as soon as possible.

- Maghira may be suffering from 'Carers' syndrome', where people who care for others do not care so effectively for themselves.

- Stress can be cumulative and/or related to specific situations.

- We can deal with stress by reducing it, temporarily or permanently, and/or by learning to cope with the pressures more effectively.

The massages were very enjoyable and did help her relax. Maghira **OUTCOME** hadn't realised how tense her body was, and she continued to be massaged, especially when her stomach pains became less and less frequent. She was also very hopeful about her week's break, but in the event it was rather disappointing. She didn't manage to go away, but had planned to have outings with her partner and Felin. Then she went down with 'flu on day two, and spent most of the week in bed. When she did get up she had no energy and couldn't do more than sit and watch films on TV — she was grateful that there were some!

Maghira went back to work feeling a bit better, but gradually began to feel that nothing fundamental had changed. The pressures were the same. She was still tired, low and increasingly frustrated. She went off to her two-day course without much hope that it would make any difference.

But this time she was pleasantly surprised. It was very helpful to have time and space to talk things over with people with similar problems. Maghira realised that she was not making use of the support she could have, and she also extended her support network by keeping in touch with one or two people from the course. On the course, she practised some relaxation techniques, from simple breathing and stretching exercises which she thought she could actually use at work, to more extensive techniques such as visualisation.

And, for the first time in a long time, she found she was having fun. She regained some perspective on her problems, and realised that work had become so important to her that other areas of life were suffering. She became determined to change this, and booked a four-week holiday (partly using accrued time-off-in-lieu) the day she returned to work. Part of her agenda for this holiday was to reconsider in depth what she wanted at work and in her personal life.

But perhaps the main thing Maghira gained was the way people's different needs were respected, and the sense of time and space to work on problems. She realised she needed to build time into her life for solitude and reflection, to keep perspective; and she understood that her needs were important — she had to take them seriously.

COMMENT *Research shows that those people who are stressed are the least well-equipped to recognise the scale of their problem and to deal with it effectively. Maghira's one-week break was not enough for the state she had reached. Nevertheless she did manage to make some improvements immediately, and to stay with the problem when her first attempts didn't 'solve' it.*

GENERAL ACTION TIPS

- Stress is a fact of life. We have to learn a variety of ways of dealing with it, and regularly review our repertoire. It is not a problem we will totally 'solve'.
- Dealing effectively with stress means taking responsibility for our own stress and working on that.
- Use a 'belt and braces' approach with stress, tackling the same problem in different ways. Plan for stressful events, to relax before, during and after.
- There is 'big deal' stress and 'small deal' stress. We need to build in relaxation strategies for both.

WHAT MAGHIRA MIGHT DO NEXT Now that she has tried some relaxation exercises and feels more positive, Maghira could learn a more in-depth method such as yoga or autonomic training. She has resolved to work with her team on how to manage the stress inherent in the work.

23 DEALING WITH STRESS IN THE TEAM

What to do when everything seems impossible

Morale at the Family Support Centre is low. With the administration post vacant, things seem less organised than usual, and the centre has not yet advertised for a replacement. Maghira has become aware of the stressfulness of her own work, and this has led her to think about the stresses inherent in the work for herself and her colleagues. She reads up a bit on organisational stress and identifies the main things that cause her stress: the conflicting demands — from communities and funders; the unpredictability of clients' demands; the inadequate resources and the huge task; the temporary problems of the bad publicity Kamlesh is orchestrating against the centre, and having no administrative support.

Should Maghira

OPTIONS

- Struggle through this temporary bad patch and try to sort things afterwards?
- Talk to the Management Committee about the problems?
- Talk to the staff about how they perceive the problems?
- Come up with a plan and try to sell it to Management Committee and staff?

TIPS on dealing with stress in the team

- Work has some inherent stresses. A common mistake is to assume that nothing can be done about these.
- Different perceptions together produce a fuller picture of the nature of the stress problems, and lead to better quality solutions.
- In dealing with stress, the earlier we tackle a problem, the smaller it is.

ACTION   Maghira has a couple of concrete ideas about cutting down on non-essential interruptions from families, and for coping without an administrator. She decides to talk to the team about these and about the problems of stress, before putting together a plan to improve things. She knows that not all the Management Committee are well disposed to her and the remaining staff, so she decides not to approach them as a whole except for actions which would require their approval. On the other hand, she has a fairly good relationship with the chair and so decides to speak privately with her *after* speaking to her team.

Pratiba, Shakti and Surinder see the merit of a rota for taking calls from clients immediately, as it means that they will only be at the mercy of the telephone for a quarter of the time each, except in cases of emergency. They reluctantly agree to Maghira's proposed division of the core administrative tasks. Pratiba suggests that they take advantage of the vacancy to re-think the administration job so it fits better with what the field worker needs — Maghira discovers that Kamlesh had sometimes been obstructive about servicing the field workers, preferring to concentrate on his 'own' work. As he had always been cooperative with her, this was news. Pratiba also raises the question of work prioritising. She says that while she can work the extra hours to cover the vacant post in the short term, in the longer term she has too many cases even *without* the extra work and she wants the Centre to think again about priorities. That is the worst stress for her. She suggests taking on no new cases for three months. Maghira's first reaction is that Pratiba is being difficult again, but she keeps this to herself, and promises to think about it. The other staff agree that there is too much work.

There is a problem with staff meetings from their point of view: they are too 'businessy', and not enough time is given to supporting each other in dealing with the families and the emotional impact of the work.

Another big issue for them is noise and lack of privacy. Each worker sometimes needs to see families in the office, and only Maghira has a private office. Surinder has priority use of a small meeting/creche room, but otherwise space is inadequate and too noisy to allow for any thinking work.

Kamlesh's smear campaign means they face some challenges from the people they work with, but they are clear that she was absolutely right to sack him. "How", says Shakti, "could we have things like that going on in the Centre when we are supposed to be about promoting healthy relationships in families?" Maghira feels supported by their firm commitment to her action.

She is surprised to discover that for them the pressures from the Management Committee, community and funders seem much less pressing. As she talks about her feelings of pressure, Surinder says, "But it's because you're so good at your job that we don't worry about all that." Pratiba suggests presenting the dilemmas back to Management Committee and funders sometimes, rather than always trying to solve the problems quickly. Maghira feels glad that she spoke about the conflicts she experiences, even though she gains no solutions.

Maghira can implement some changes at once, and begin to plan for **OUTCOME** some others. She gets the treasurer's approval to engage a part-time locum secretary. She and the staff review the administrator role so that it is more geared to servicing the fieldwork team; it is then advertised. She negotiates with the Treasurer (an old ally) to take on a bigger role in overseeing month-to-month finances for the rest of the year.

Maghira gets a one-off underspend grant to enlarge the reception area and improve connections between it and the main work room, so that the administrator and whoever is 'on call' can be based there. This makes the main room much quieter, and together the team work out a furniture arrangement that balances privacy and safety better. Maghira offers the use of her office to other staff on the two mornings a week she is out, and a rota is negotiated with Surinder to give the others more access to the meeting/creche room.

While she does not feel it is a good time to stop taking new cases or persuade the Management Committee to re-prioritise, Maghira starts to work with the team to identify the issues that should be considered in prioritising, so that the groundwork has been done when a more propitious moment arises. She also takes Pratiba's advice to heart, and begins to think how to present her role conflict to Management Committee and funders, so that she no longer bears the burden of decision all alone.

Maghira decides to use a standard agenda for staff meetings which allows for discussion of cases and mutual support. She also takes up Surinder's suggestion of a weekly 'wind-down' session where the team can discuss their feelings about the work. Surinder is doing a groupwork course in her own time and offers to facilitate this session.

There are no once-for-all solutions to stress at work, as the world in which **COMMENT** *we operate changes constantly. Maghira and her staff found some positive concrete measures to improve their situation, and provide each other with needed support.*

GENERAL ACTION TIPS

- Some stress at work is individual, and some is related to the work and its demands; different strategies are needed for each. A manager may have different stresses arising from a different role.

- Problems arising from physical conditions can be tackled, often without spending a fortune.

- It costs only time to help staff deal with the emotional impact of the work.

WHAT MAGHIRA MIGHT DO NEXT She might research the possibility of moving premises, and funding such a move; she could lay the groundwork with sympathetic Management Committee members for a thorough-going review of the Centre's priorities. She could review with staff the success of the measures taken and plan for some further measures.

24 COMPLAINTS ABOUT AN EMPLOYEE'S WORK

Taking a cool appraisal without losing your cool

Carla has had a complaint about one of her health promotion workers, David. He was due to go to a mixed sixth form at a local school to give a film and presentation about contraception and distribute some follow up materials for use by the class teacher in general studies sessions. The head teacher has phoned to say that:

- David was late.
- He couldn't work the video.
- The class disintegrated into giggles and catcalls and he had no idea how to regain control.
- He forgot the follow up material.

The head is annoyed and gives Carla an earbashing. More seriously he says he may complain to the local Health Education Council. Carla slams down the phone and sits at her desk seething.

Should Carla: OPTIONS

- Storm out and find David now and give him an earful like she's just had in front of the rest of the staff?
- Wait until she's calmed down a bit and then spring it on him in private?
- Tell him she wants to see him after lunch about the visit to the school as she's had a complaint?

Carla does some deep breathing, checks her work plan and David's and **PLANNING** leaves a note for David to say she must see him promptly after lunch re trip to the school.

She knows David is not usually slapdash or a poor worker but feels this is a sufficiently worrying level of complaint to go into in some depth.

She sets aside an hour for the meeting and tells David her time schedule.

TIPS on feedback

- Give feedback (positive or negative) as soon as the situation arises.

- Don't pass on other people's anger or annoyance about the problem. The earbashing the head gave Carla may not be fair or diplomatic, but it's not good practice to pass it on either — certainly not in front of the rest of the staff.

- If you receive a negative comment about someone's work or performance from a third party check out the situation or event from the worker concerned first.

- Wait until you are calm before giving feedback or checking out the facts.

OPTIONS Carla is now feeling stressed and pressured to get on with her grant application that has to be done now, but keeps getting replays of the annoying phone call from the head and her annoyance with David.

Should she:

- Work on regardless, ignore her emotions and get on with the grant application?
- Go and have a second cup of coffee and a walk in the hospital car park?
- Prepare for 10 minutes for her meeting with David and get it out of her head?

TIPS on difficult meetings

- Preparing for any meeting or negotiation that you feel may be 'difficult' is important.

- Carla will have to do this preparation anyway and so may as well do it now and get it out of her head and stopping her from concentrating.

Carla prepares for her meeting. She lists the complaints from the head   **ACTION**
teacher and thinks about the outcomes she wants:

- reassurance that this is not a normal occurrence
- to go over the head teacher's points
- better service delivery in future
- a mollified head teacher.

She plans how to handle the meeting:

- she will present the issue neutrally
- ask David's version and reasons
- decide together with David on short-term and long-term action as a
  result.

Now she can get on with her grant application.

Carla handled a difficult interruption to her work schedule well and **COMMENT**
prevented it from distracting her further by planning it and shelving it to the
appropriate time.

Read up on 'Giving Feedback'.   **WHAT CARLA**
                                                                 MIGHT DO
                                                                 NEXT

GENERAL ACTION TIPS

- Don't rush in and confront someone when you're in a bad
  mood and feel like lynching them. You won't get better
  motivated staff next time or hear their side of the story.
- Plan for difficult meetings and you can then concentrate on
  the words and interpersonal relationship in the meeting
  rather than the shape or plan of the meeting.
- Don't have expectations about what the outcome of the
  dialogue will be. Allow them to respond to you rather
  than having a preprepared 'script' in your head.

---

25 FORMAL DISCIPLINARY INTERVIEWS

What to do when good management doesn't work

Simon has been working with one of his energy advisers, Carlos on his drink problem, that has been affecting his conduct. They drew up a formal contract for improvement over a month. Carlos has made some improvement, and has attended one counselling session. For two weeks he did not appear to be drinking. Simon has now heard that when he was out of the office on Friday, Robina saw Carlos have three pints in the pub across the road at lunchtime. That afternoon he did very little work and fell asleep at his desk at 3.00pm. He was rude and belligerent with Robina when she tackled him, and called her 'an interfering cow' and left.

Carlos apologised to her on the following Monday, but has been very withdrawn and has hardly spoken to the other staff or Simon. Robina has not made a formal complaint.

OPTIONS **Should Simon:**

- Take Carlos aside for an informal discussion about what happened on Friday and why?
- Phone the chair of the Management Committee and discuss what to do?
- Interview Carlos formally and immediately issue a formal written warning?

TIPS on disciplinary interviews

- Take a balance between understanding the employee's difficulties and the need to take a professional approach to work and working relationships.
- Stick to the contract drawn up for improvement of work.
- Follow formal disciplinary proceedings.

96

Simon checks through the contract agreed with Carlos for improving his **ACTION**
performance, and decides it is time to review it anyway. He rereads the
disciplinary procedure and decides that he should follow it and issue a
formal notice of a disciplinary panel. Before he does anything else he
phones the chair of the Management Committee to discuss his
impending action.

He drafts his letter to Carlos, checks it with the chair and issues it later
that day. He calls Carlos into his office to explain why he is issuing it,
informs him of the date for the formal meeting and reminds him that he
can have his union representative present if he so wishes.

Simon then gathers all the necessary information: the contract with
Carlos, the minutes of that meeting, a written statement from Robina,
and the letter about the disciplinary meeting. He encourages Carlos to
write down his side of the story.

Simon convenes the discipline and grievance panel meeting with the
Secretary of the Management Committee, another committee member,
Carlos and a union representative. They go through the notes of the first
meeting and Robina's report of the recent incident.

Carlos explains that his drinking was the result of a difficult meeting he
had had with a council environmental worker that morning. He
regretted the incident and that he was rude to Robina for which he
apologised.

The contract Simon drew up with him when the drinking problem was
first discovered, specified the following points:

1. Carlos must seek counselling on his drinking problems.

2. Carlos must not drink alcohol at lunchtimes when he is at work.

3. Carlos must not come into work so incapacitated that his work is poor.

Simon points out that he has broken his contract on two counts — points
1 and 3 — and asks about the counselling. Carlos says that the stress
counsellor was no good and he hadn't been back to her. Meanwhile the
situation at home was still very stressful.

The union representative says that Carlos has tried to keep to his contract
but that he had been expected to work under intolerable levels of stress.
He said that his drinking behaviour had been generally good, and it was
only this isolated lapse that had been a problem in the whole month.
Simon reported that his morale was not good, but agreed that it was only
one incident in the whole month.

OUTCOME The Panel decided to issue Carlos with a written warning that any further conduct that breaches the agreement will lead to a final written warning or possibly dismissal depending on the seriousness of the breach. They specify that:

- Carlos must attend stress counselling.

- He must keep to the first contract.

- He is given a week off to try and sort out some of the symptoms of stress and have a breather.

A review date of a further month is set.

Formal notes of the meeting are written and agreed by all parties as a true record of the meeting.

COMMENT *The panel have been fair, but issued further strict guidelines about Carlos' expected behaviour. They have also recognised that he needs time to sort himself out and have granted time for him to do this.*

GENERAL ACTION TIPS

- Check the terms of the disciplinary procedure and stick to them.
- Make sure all written minutes or notes of standards agreed are kept and agreed by all parties.
- Keep the interview fair and formal.

WHAT SIMON MIGHT DO NEXT Make sure he knows what Carlos is up to and checks his work performance.

DEALING WITH DIFFICULT SITUATIONS

GENERAL

VOLUNTARY BUT NOT AMATEUR, D Forbes, R Hayes & J Reason, London Voluntary Service Council, 1994, £12.95

Offers model conditions of service.

SENSITIVE ISSUES IN THE WORKPLACE, Sue Morris, Industrial Society, 1994

Good basic introduction to sensitive issues and management.

BULLYING AT WORK: How to confront and overcome it., Andrea Adams, Virago, 1992

MANAGING ABSENCE, C Morton, S Hargreaves & G Taylor, Russell House Publishing, 1998 (forthcoming), £14.95

HARASSMENT

WOMEN AND HARASSMENT AT WORK, Nathalie Hadjifotiou, Pluto Press, 1984

SEXUAL HARASSMENT AT WORK: a TUC guide for trade unionists, TUC, 1983

NO OFFENSE? SEXUAL HARASSMENT: how it happens and how to beat it, Industrial Society, 1993

SEXUAL HARASSMENT — Information pack from the EOC.

DISCIPLINARY AND GRIEVANCE PROCEDURES

DISCIPLINARY PRACTICE AND PROCEDURES IN EMPLOYMENT: Code of Practice 1, Advisory Conciliation and Arbitration Service. Available through TSO bookshops, £1.90, ISBN 0 11 88 50 008.

Essential features of disciplinary procedures and recommendations for use.

GUIDE TO DISCIPLINE, Croner's Employment Law Editorial Department, Croner, 1988, £6.60.

Addresses problems managers face complying with legal requirements.

THE VOLUNTARY SECTOR LEGAL HANDBOOK, S Adirondack & J Sinclair Taylor, Directory of Social Change, 1996, £35.00 (voluntary organisations), £50 (others)

RACIAL DISCRIMINATION AND GRIEVANCE PROCEDURES, CRE, 1992 £1.00.

A practical guide for employers.

EMPLOYMENT PRACTICE IN THE VOLUNTARY SECTOR, Brent Voluntary Service Council, 1984.

Includes disciplinary and grievance procedure.

GUIDE TO FAIR DISMISSAL, Croner's Employment Law Editorial Department, Croner, 1987, £6.60.

Guide to relevant statutes covering principles of unfair dismissal law.

HIV AND AIDS

AIDS AND EMPLOYMENT — booklet from the HSE and Employment Department, The Mailing House, Leeland Rd, London W13 9HL.

HELPLINE, Terrence Higgins Trust, 0171-242 1010 12–10pm daily.

STRESS

STRESS AND RELAXATION, Jane Madders, MacDonald Optima, 1988, £6.99 from bookshops.

COPING WITH STRESS: a practical self-help guide for women, Georgina Witkin-Lanoil, Sheldon Press, 1987, £3.99.

BEATING JOB BURNOUT, Dr Donald Scott, Sheldon Press, 1989 £3.99.

USEFUL ORGANISATIONS

COMMISSION FOR RACIAL EQUALITY, Elliot House, 10–12 Allington Street, London SW1E 5EH. *Tel:* 0171-828 7022.

EQUAL OPPORTUNITIES COMMISSION, Overseas House, Quay Street, Manchester M3 3HN. *Tel:* 0161-833 9244.

Section 4

MANAGEMENT COMMITTEE

Scenarios

26 FACTIONS ON THE Management Committee

Facing up to division and strife on the governing body

The Family Support Centre has sacked Kamlesh for sexual harassment. The Chair and executive (Chair, Treasurer and two other Management Committee members) made the decision, but some members of the committee feel that Kamlesh should have been given 'another chance', and two are his active supporters — one of them, Rory, is related to his wife. They feel that Maghira acted beyond her authority, and that she and her staff are too influenced by values from outside the community, and are rampant feminists who want to break up traditional values. While the rest of the committee don't see things quite like this, many of them are concerned that traditional values be preserved. A number of people are talking very freely outside the centre about their concerns. The last committee meeting was awful, although the executive's decision to dismiss Kamlesh was (narrowly) approved.

Maghira and Harbinder, the Chair, are concerned. They want to stop the gossip, protect the centre's interests by putting the episode in the past, and get everyone pulling in the same direction.

OPTIONS Should Maghira and Harbinder:

- Ignore the issue at the next meeting, and concentrate on future planning?
- Order everyone to stop gossiping?
- Forbid Rory to speak, on the basis that as Kamlesh's wife's uncle he has a conflict of interests?
- Allow a free-for-all?

PLANNING Maghira and Harbinder plan the next meeting carefully. It is agreed that Maghira will keep a low profile, and that after some quick and unimportant items, the first major item should be how to deal with the aftermath of Kamlesh's dismissal. Harbinder will state the position and set some ground rules, to give a context for people to contribute.

TIPS on handling meetings

- In a situation where feelings are running high, it is seldom a good idea to ignore the issue totally. But careful structuring is required, so that things don't get out of hand.

- Issues of authority between staff and Management Committee are common. Although Maghira kept the Chair informed and involved, and her decision to dismiss was approved by the executive, the decision is being seen as hers and is being challenged on that basis — that she exceeded her authority.

- Maghira's position at the committee meeting will be quite isolated. It is important that the Chair take responsibility in her role for the decision, both to protect and support Maghira, and to re-address the committee to its role.

The item opens well. Everyone has arrived and is waiting expectantly. **ACTION** Harbinder recaps what has happened, emphasising that the decision to dismiss was made by the executive and approved by the committee at its last meeting. She says that she is concerned that gossip may damage the centre, both with users and with funders. She says that now the decision has been made and carried out, she now wants everyone to put the past behind. She will now allow some time for a final discussion of the lessons learnt; a collective statement about the issue should then be agreed, and at the end of the item she will ask each person for an individual commitment to stick to that in what they say outside.

Things start out quite well, with agreement that a policy is needed and statements of support for Harbinder and Maghira for the professional way they have handled the problem. Then Rory begins to speak, and after a while Harbinder realises that he is trying to re-run the debate about whether or not Kamlesh should have been dismissed, and arguing for his re-instatement!

At this point she intervenes, saying that the decision is already made, and that she believes it to have been the correct one; however even if it had been the wrong decision, to re-instate now would totally undermine Maghira and her staff. Then Kamlesh's other supporter weighs in, accusing Harbinder of being in league with Maghira to 'undermine the authority of the man in the family'. He continues in this vein for a few minutes before Harbinder succeeds in interrupting him — actually by shouting him down.

Harbinder makes it clear that it is not OK to abuse others in the meeting. Calling out that it is all a cover-up for a feminist plot, the two men storm out of the meeting. Harbinder is absolutely furious, but she proposes a break at this point for everyone to calm themselves.

OUTCOME When the meeting resumes the tone is much calmer, indeed it is hard to detect much difference of opinion at all. There are many expressions of support for Harbinder; the feeling is that she has been unjustly attacked — indeed Harbinder herself was so angry because she holds rather traditional views and does not see herself in any way as a 'feminist' — her disagreements with Maghira are often about this issue. Harbinder asks what should be done about the two people who walked out, but the general attitude seems to be that if they choose to leave, the committee should confirm their resignation. Harbinder agrees to write to them to do this. She has no difficulty in getting a 'party line' agreed on Kamlesh's dismissal, and in getting each person to say that they will say nothing else about the matter to anyone outside the committee.

COMMENT *The meeting is only partially successful, as agreement is achieved only after two members have withdrawn. When a situation is as polarised as this one, the chances of a reconciliation — of Harbinder holding the committee together — are not high. It is just possible that things would not have become so heated if she had simply said that the decision to dismiss was final, rather than going into the reasons why it must remain final.*

Harbinder successfully protected Maghira by her strong stance, which drew the fire of the disgruntled members onto herself. Ironically their abuse had the effect of uniting everyone else behind her, since no one could see Harbinder as a 'feminist plotter'. Other factions were, at least temporarily, dissolved.

Something to watch out for here are elements of scapegoating and false consensus. After Rory and his friend have left, agreement is easy to achieve, despite a broad spectrum of views remaining on the committee. Although the decision to allow them to leave may be correct, it is arrived at too easily; it is as though indignation with the two men afterwards robs others of the right to express dissenting views. This temporary sinking of differences, however, has a positive side; as long as disagreement can now be expressed and worked with, the committee now has an opportunity to move forward. All in all, Harbinder and Maghira have got what they wanted from the meeting.

GENERAL ACTION TIPS

- It is useful to remind people of their collective responsibility.
- And to ask them to take individual responsibility for it.
- Challenge abuse, but try not to take it personally.
- Remember there is no 'perfect' outcome.

WHAT HARBINDER AND MAGHIRA MIGHT DO NEXT

They need to continue to monitor for gossip, and must replace the members they have lost; Harbinder should work to help committee members to express and work through differing views on other issues.

27 GETTING MORE MEMBERS ON THE COMMITTEE

Recruiting skilled and committed people

Maghira and Harbinder are meeting to review the last Management Committee meeting. After losing two people in a violent row, the Family Centre's committee needs to recruit some more members. They are discussing how best to do this.

OPTIONS Should Maghira and Harbinder:

- Invite some likely people along to the next meeting?
- Advertise?
- Contact some local community organisations to send nominees?

TIPS on finding people for the committee

All the above are possible ways of finding people but Maghira realises that the problem at the moment is that she and Harbinder don't really agree about who is needed. She wants some more people who have experience of managing staff and of actually working with families, whereas Harbinder is keen to increase community, and if possible user, representation.

- The first step is to agree what people you want.
- The next to identify where they are and how you might contact and interest them.
- Don't forget to think about what their induction and support needs might be.

ACTION Maghira and Harbinder agree that people with *all* the skills and experience they have identified between them, are needed. Given the present fragile state of the committee, they think it would be a bad idea to invite anyone along at present — it might put them off, and certainly would run the risk of annoying some of the present members.

106

They decide to present their list of skills and experience to the committee, making it clear that they think three or four people will need to be recruited. They each have one or two people they think might be interested, and agree to approach them informally. They decide to ask committee members whom else they think is needed, and whether they know any suitable people.

Harbinder has an induction pack used by new staff and committee members in the organisation where she works. She is very keen for the Family Centre to have one. Maghira privately thinks that it would be a lot of work to produce, but agrees that it is useful, particularly for less confident or experienced committee members.

At the next meeting, Harbinder states the problem: that the remaining eight members of the committee cannot do all the work necessary, so that new members are needed. She adds that she would like to strengthen participation by the communities the centre serves, from the present three members, to four or five. She reminds the committee that it is their responsibility to ensure that they have enough members to do the work.

The discussion takes a while to get going, but Harbinder chairs it very patiently, and keeps re-addressing members to the issue. Someone says that he thinks more people with financial skills are needed. Several people support the idea of an induction pack, saying that they would have become active on the committee more quickly if they had had a summary of key information at the start. Someone points out that if the pack is put on computer, it can easily be updated. Maghira is surprised to notice that two funders' representatives are saying this, so it isn't just those who have little experience who find the information helpful!

Maghira agrees to make a proposal at the next meeting about how work **OUTCOME** might be re-scheduled so that a pack could be produced quickly. One committee member offers to help produce it, as he says it would help him to learn.

Members know one or two more people who might be interested in joining the committee, and someone agrees to contact two community associations to see whether they might send a nominee. It is suggested that a special meeting and social event could be held for people who are interested, to meet the staff and find out a bit more about the organisation. If this were done in the next month, anyone who then wanted to could be nominated in time to stand for the committee at the AGM. Harbinder suggests that it would be a good idea to have food at this event, and a member, who rarely speaks at the meetings, offers to organise some.

COMMENT *By putting the problem, rather than any solution to the committee, Harbinder and Maghira successfully involved the committee members in trying to solve it. They may still have difficulty finding the right people, but there are more of them working on the problem, and working together on it together is good experience for the people who are already there.*

GENERAL ACTION TIPS

- In a charity, keeping the numbers up is the *committee's* legal responsibility.

- The constitution will normally state how committee members should be appointed or elected. Remember to bear these parameters in mind.

- Good chairing allows time for people to find their own solutions.

- Look for opportunities to strengthen the existing group in working together, and for ways for people to contribute.

- A special meeting may be more accessible than an ordinary committee meeting for people coming to see whether or not they want to get more involved.

WHAT HARBINDER AND MAGHIRA MIGHT DO NEXT Make up the induction pack; consider the training needs of committee members, individually and collectively; consider team-building for the committee.

28 RELATIONS WITH THE Management Committee

Understanding and developing a sense of partnership

Maghira has a recurring problem with her Management Committee over issues of power and authority; at the meetings some people constantly question whether or not she has done the right thing, made the right decision, or whether she had the right to make the decision. This has come up again recently over dismissing Kamlesh, but has happened many times before. Maghira is very clear about lines of authority and believes that she is generally acting within her own; she resents the interference. Now one member has taken to calling unannounced at the centre, in order to give her instructions (he calls this 'line management'). Maghira is furious she feels she could work a lot more efficiently with no committee at all.

Should Maghira: OPTIONS

- Tell the member who is behaving inappropriately to get lost?
- Refer the matter to the committee?
- Try to tackle the root problem?

TIPS on relations with the Management Committee

- If a problem keeps coming up, it is more effective and more efficient to tackle its root causes.
- In dealing with issues of authority, it is important to preserve everyone's dignity.
- It is important to insist on being treated with respect, as well as treating others with respect.
- Use established lines of authority if possible to tackle the problem.

ACTION   Maghira takes a few deep breaths, and remembers that she has a pretty good relationship with Harbinder, the Chair of her Management Committee, although they certainly have their differences.   She telephones Harbinder and tells her about the problem, saying she wants it raised at the next committee meeting.   Harbinder agrees to speak privately to the member, making it clear that she is Maghira's line manager. She feels this will minimise his loss of face.

Maghira feels that there is a more underlying problem about the lack of respect with which the committee treats her.   She doesn't think that all the members understand how responsible her job is, and some are inclined to treat her like a minion.

Harbinder agrees that not everyone on the committee understands the work of the centre, and adds that she thinks it would be helpful for members to meet other staff too, to get more idea of the work. (Maghira remembers that she had intended to involve the others more, but hasn't yet done it.)   Harbinder suggests that they have a meeting of staff and Management Committee members to clarify the roles and responsibilities of each; Maghira thinks this might be a good idea, and says that she knows someone in social services who might facilitate the meeting for them.   She is pretty sure the staff will be quite keen.   Maghira feels glad she rang Harbinder, because Harbinder does take her responsibility seriously and will always tackle problems, even if not always in the way Maghira wants.

OUTCOME   At the next committee meeting, Harbinder says that there is an issue about the line management of the project staff which it is important to clarify. She says that it was decided two years ago (before most of the present committee joined) that she should line-manage Maghira, who in turn line-manages the other staff.   Harbinder is accountable for her management first to the executive, and then to the full Management Committee.

She suggests that it might be useful for the committee to clarify with staff what their relative roles and responsibilities are.   One person doesn't see the point, but then several others agree with Harbinder.   One suggests tying this process in with a review of the work and making a day of it. This is agreed.

COMMENT   *Maghira alerted Harbinder to the specific problem, which was dealt with quickly and sensitively.   Harbinder then clarified the line management position to the committee in general, and suggested a way forward which could improve communication considerably in the future.   It was again*

110

Harbinder who was the better person to raise the issue with the committee, because of her role as Chair, and because she was not directly involved in the problem.

GENERAL ACTION TIPS

- Deal with the symptoms of a problem, but don't stop there: if there is an underlying problem, tackle it.
- Improving relationships can best be achieved by getting the agreement of all concerned to a process.
- Poor relationships are much less often the result of 'personality clash' than we might think. Unclear boundaries or roles are a prime cause of tension.
- Despite differences in values and approach, Harbinder and Maghira work effectively together, because they respect each other.

Arrange for more opportunities for the committee to meet staff and become familiar with the work, within the boundaries agreed.

WHAT HARBINDER AND MAGHIRA MIGHT DO NEXT

MORE INFORMATION ON:

Management Committee

GETTING ORGANISED, Christine Holloway & Shirley Otto, Bedford Square Press, 1986, £5.95.

Ideas to improve the meetings and decision making of Management Committees.

JUST ABOUT MANAGING, Sandy Adirondack, London Voluntary Service Council, 1998, £12.45.

Practical guide to good management in voluntary organisations and community groups.

THE TRUSTEE ORGANISER, Directory of Social Change, 1993, £12.50

Ring binder with practical information for trustees, as well as space to file minutes of meetings, committee papers etc.

THE EFFECTIVE TRUSTEE, Kevin Ford, Directory of Social Change, 1993.

> Part 1: Roles and responsibilities, £7.95
> Part 2: Aims and resources, £7.95
> Part 3: Getting the work done, £7.95

THE GOOD TRUSTEE GUIDE: a resource organiser for members of governing bodies of charitable companies, National Council for Voluntary Organisations, £11.95.

HELPING PEOPLE WORK TOGETHER, R. Douglas et al, National Institute for Social Work, 1988, £6.00.

Gives practical tools to help voluntary groups carry out tasks efficiently and creatively.

THE COMMITTEE BOOK, Audrie Stratford, Foulsham & Co, 1988, £4.99.

Examines the roles and duties of committee members and looks at official decision making.

COMPANY SECRETARIAL PRACTICE, Institute of Chartered Secretaries and Administrators, 1988, £125.00 + £2.00 p+p.

Looks at the procedures of formal meetings and the role of committee members.

MANAGING VOLUNTARY ORGANISATIONS AND COMMUNITY GROUPS, Islington Voluntary Action Council, 1985.

Checklist looking at all areas of Management Committees — aimed at Management Committee members.

FACING CLOSURE, Karen Mackay, Federation of Independent Advice Centres, 1986, £1.00.

Looks at Management Committee liabilities in the face of financial crisis.

THE MANAGER'S HANDBOOK, A. Young, Sphere, 1989, £12.95.

Examines various aspects in achieving successful management.

MANAGING TO ADVISE, Christine Thornton, Federation of Independent Advice Centres, 1995 (revised edition).

Chapter on Management Committee organisation.

USEFUL ORGANISATION

NCVO TRUSTEE UNIT, National Council for Voluntary Organisations, Regent's Wharf, 8 All Saints Road, London N1 9RL. *Tel:* 0171-713 6161.

Information and advice on trustee matters.

Section 5

LETTING STAFF GO IN DIFFICULT CIRCUMSTANCES

29 DISMISSAL

What to do if everything else has failed?

It is now two months since Carlos' first written warning was issued concerning his work performance and his drinking. Unfortunately he has failed to keep to his contract twice and has been issued with a final written warning two weeks ago. Today he has phoned in sick at 1pm in the afternoon, obviously drunk and not really coherent. Simon gets the message and feels angry with Carlos for making a mess of the contract, but mainly saddened that he has little choice about how to proceed.

OPTIONS Should Simon:

- Phone the chair of the Management Committee to discuss what to do?
- Issue a dismissal letter himself straight away?
- Phone Carlos back and tell him not to bother coming in?

TIPS on dismissal

- Taking action to dismiss someone is always a serious step: make sure you act formally and correctly.
- Stick to the disciplinary procedure.
- Always discuss such a serious step with the chair of the Management Committee.

PLANNING Simon:

- Checks the legal position — see overleaf.
- Checks the disciplinary procedure.
- Phones the chair of the Management Committee.

Simon drafts the letter of dismissal outlining the reasons why Carlos is **ACTION**
being dismissed and the period of notice Carlos is entitled to. This will
be the amount of time specified in the contract or the minimum amount
specified by law. Or the organisation can offer Carlos pay in lieu of
notice if they don't want him to continue to work there during the notice
period.

The letter must mention the right of appeal internal to the organisation.

It is necessary to decide if you want the worker to go straight away or **COMMENT**
whether they can stay and work out their notice. This time period is likely
to be very uncomfortable!

In this case it would be better to offer pay in lieu of notice as Carlos is not
likely to improve his conduct after such a long time of trying to improve
and not succeeding.

GENERAL ACTION TIPS

- There is no point in putting off the inevitable: once you
  have decided what to do then do it.
- Always check the text of final written warnings or
  dismissals with the Management Committee chair as they
  are the legal employers.
- If you act according to principles laid down by ACAS and
  follow your disciplinary procedure then you will probably
  be deemed to have acted fairly.
- Keep all documentation in case of appeals.

Sacking someone is always difficult. He could relax and follow stress **WHAT SIMON**
reduction techniques outlined in Scenarios 22 and 23 (pages 86–92). **MIGHT DO**
NEXT

LEGAL INFORMATION ON DISMISSAL

If the worker has been employed for less than two years, they have no right to claim unfair dismissal based on conduct and can be dismissed without reasons being given.

If the worker has been working for two years or more (full time or part time) they can claim unfair dismissal if they feel they have been unfairly dismissed (within a time limit of 3 months). The employer would have to show evidence (where relevant) that:

- The employee is unable to do the work for which they were employed.
- The employee is unwilling to do the work.
- The employee has continued to break rules even after warnings.
- There was gross misconduct.
- The disciplinary procedures were followed.
- The procedures conform to ACAS guidelines. (Advisory Conciliation and Arbitration Service, *tel:* 0171-210 3000.)

DRINKING

Dismissals relating to an employee's drinking whether on or off duty are potentially fair, provided they have been handled fairly and in line with appropriate procedures.

CAPABILITY

Where an employee is suffering from a chronic alcoholism, they should be treated as any other employee with a medical condition. The fairness of the dismissal will therefore depend on the employer's establishing the true medical condition and giving the employee a reasonable time in which to recover.

CAPACITY

If an employee commits an isolated act related to drink or breaches an organisation rule or policy by being under the influence of drink at work then, provided the proper disciplinary procedures have been followed, dismissal will be seen to be fair.

APPEAL

Where the organisation has an appeal procedure then the worker has the right to know about it and use it. If the appeal procedure confirms the dismissal, the effective date of dismissal is the date originally given.

The employee still has the right to go to an industrial tribunal if they think they have been unfairly dismissed. All employees have the right to written reasons for dismissal after continuous service of two years.

It is automatically unfair to dismiss for the following reasons:

- trade union activities or membership or non membership
- pregnancy
- sex or race
- a spent conviction under the rehabilitation of Offenders Act
- taking appropriate action for health and safety reasons
- on the transfer of a company under the transfer of undertakings regulations where transfer is the main reason for dismissal.

30 REDUNDANCY

What to do if someone on the staff has to go

Maghira has received a notice from the council cutting their grant by £20,000. All voluntary sector projects have received cuts and she has already been to appeals and protests about it from the voluntary sector group. There is no way out of it. Someone will have to be made redundant. One of the full-time workers would save £20,000. Only one has been in post long enough to get redundancy money (2 years).

OPTIONS **Should Maghira**

- Select one of the workers who won't need paying redundancy money?
- Select the newest member of staff?
- Consult with the Management Committee and staff on the situation?

TIPS on redundancy

When facing redundancy there are certain steps that have to be taken by law.

- Consultation must take place with employees' representatives and unions recognised for negotiation purposes.
- This must begin at the earliest opportunity when there is a proposal to make redundancies:

  — for between 10 and 100 employees the minimum consultation time is 30 days

  — for less than 10 employees 28 days is a suggested time guide.

- Employees do not qualify for redundancy if they are offered suitable alternative employment, are guilty of misconduct, or are working under a fixed-term contract and have waived redundancy rights. *(continued overleaf)*

120

More TIPS on redundancy

- Employers are obliged to select for redundancy on grounds which are non discriminatory on grounds of sex, race or trade union membership.
- Employees have the right to reasonable time off to look for other work, to notice and to redundancy pay.
- To qualify for redundancy pay employees must have been employed for two years by the date of dismissal regardless of number of hours worked per week.
- Redundancy pay is calculated on what terms are offered in the contract or on statutory redundancy which is calculated on the workers age and length of employment.

  For example, for each year of service between the ages of 22 and 41 the employee receives one week's pay (up to a maximum of £205 per week).

PLANNING

Maghira reads up on the conditions for redundancy in her Personnel Management guidebook. She can't offer any suitable alternative work because there isn't any!

She organises an emergency meeting of the Management Committee to discuss what to do, before saying anything to the staff team. She presents the Management Committee with the facts of redundancy and the options before them.

The Management Committee are reluctant to come to any decision without first having consulted staff.

ACTION

As soon after the Management Committee have met as possible she calls a staff meeting and explains the situation. They discuss if other funds could be found in time and how they might try to raise them. At the worst outcome one worker has to be made redundant. She asks people to think about it and if there are any volunteers for redundancy or if workers would be prepared to work shorter hours to keep all staff in post. She then explains that if anyone is to be made redundant one person will have to be selected from the outreach workers. Pratibha has been in post for one year and does not qualify for redundancy pay. Shakti has been in post for three years and does qualify for redundancy pay of 3 x £205 = £615.

OUTCOME Staff are not prepared to work shorter hours and neither of the outreach workers volunteers for redundancy. Maghira decides that whoever is made redundant should get the same redundancy pay as Shakti, so that no one gets less than the other. She decides in consultation with the Management Committee that Shakti will be made redundant as she has less diverse language skills than Pratibha and will be able to provide a less comprehensive outreach service on her own than Pratibha would.

She breaks the news as sensitively as she can to Shakti, offers counselling and time off to look for other work, and advice on where to find another job.

COMMENT *This situation is very difficult for any organisation, but especially where you have to decide between two very similarly skilled workers. Maghira made the decision on the grounds of strategic use to the organisation which is fair and has offered an equal amount of pay so that monetary loss to the organisation did not affect the decision.*

GENERAL ACTION TIPS

- It is not legal to select part-timers over full-timers or one particular race or sex for redundancy in a discriminatory way. The guidance is to follow the normal procedures! However in small voluntary organisations there rarely are 'normal' procedures.

- Employees' claims based on unfair selection have succeeded where the employer failed to follow an agreed procedure on redundancies or failed to follow a 'last in first out' rule where this was customary. However the Employment Appeal Tribunal has ruled that ultimately employers have managerial control over whom to select and that tribunals should not question their decision unless there are good reasons for doing so. Nevertheless, employers must be prepared to explain the reasons for the selection and provide evidence.

- Insufficient warning of impending redundancy, lack of individual consultation with employees soon to be made redundant and failure to investigate thoroughly the possibilities of other employment before deciding to dismiss can all make the manner of implementing the redundancy unfair.

Sample policy on selection for redundancy

- When selecting for redundancy we will treat all staff equally and on the same basis, irrespective of length of service, part-time or full-time employment, or any other factor not related to the post they fill.
- Redundancies will only be made in line with the strategic plan.
- We will not impose across the board cuts in pay or hours.
- No staff will be made redundant in order for their post to be filled by a volunteer or a succession of volunteers. Specific tasks appropriate to volunteers may, however, be reallocated to them.

In future it might be worth banding together with other community groups to lobby for no cuts in funding and access to alternative sources of funds from the council.

WHAT MAGHIRA MIGHT DO NEXT

LETTING STAFF GO IN DIFFICULT CIRCUMSTANCES

MODEL DISCIPLINARY AND GRIEVANCE PROCEDURES

DISCIPLINARY PRACTICE AND PROCEDURES IN EMPLOYMENT: Code of Practice 1, Advisory Conciliation and Arbitration Service. Available through TSO bookshops, £1.90, ISBN 0 11 88 50 008

Essential features of disciplinary procedures and how to use them.

YOUR LEGAL RESPONSIBILITIES AS AN EMPLOYER

RACIAL HARASSMENT AT WORK: What employers can do about it, Commission for Racial Equality, 1995, £5.00. Available from Central books *Tel:* 0181 986 5488 .

Explains what unlawful discrimination is and how to act against it.

PREGNANT AT WORK, Maternity Alliance, 1997, £1.00

Leaflet that goes through the legal rights of pregnant women at work.

EMPLOYEE'S RIGHTS ON INSOLVENCY OF EMPLOYER, 1986, free. Available from Department for Education and Employment order line, *Tel:* 0845 602 2260.

Explains how to claim for compensation from an insolvent employer.

CRONER'S reference guides

*Various handbooks, with an updating service as the law changes, available in reference libraries and many councils for voluntary service. Also **GUIDE TO FAIR DISMISSAL**, 1987, £9.50.*

THE PERSONNEL MANAGER'S FACTBOOK, GEE Publishing Ltd, £225 for 1st year, £205 for updates, updated four times a year.

Similar to the above covering all aspects of employment law.

USEFUL ORGANISATION

ADVISORY CONCILIATION AND ARBITRATION SERVICE, Brandon House, 180 Borough High Street, London SE1 1LW. *Tel:* 01455 852225.